Indian Lowfat

COOKING

Indian Lowfat
COOKING

THE KEY TO A HEALTHY
AND EXOTIC DIET

ROSHI RAZZAQ

CHARTWELL
BOOKS, INC.

A QUINTET BOOK

Published by Chartwell Books
A Division of Book Sales, Inc.
110 Enterprise Avenue
Secaucus, New Jersey 07094

ISBN 1-55521-898-9

This book was designed and produced by
Quintet Publishing Limited
6 Blundell Street, London N7 9BH

Creative Director: Richard Dewing
Designer: Chris Dymond
Project Editor: Stefanie Foster
Editor: Michelle Clark
Photographer: Trevor Wood
Home Economist: Judith Kelsey

Dedication
To my mother, Altaf, who constantly tried to share
the secrets of her culinary arts with her daughters,
and was always under the impression that I was not
really listening . . .

Typeset in Great Britain by
Central Southern Typesetters, Eastbourne
Manufactured in Singapore by
J. Film Process Pte Ltd
Printed in Hong Kong by
Leefung-Asco Printers Limited

Contents

Introduction

Image and tradition

I remember reading somewhere that food in most Indian restaurants is so fattening that just by walking past one you are likely to put on weight.

It is not Indian food which is at fault here but the way it is mostly prepared. Indian cuisine is very flexible with the consumption of fat – there are no set rules. There is always room to add, if you like, a bit more, without changing the taste of a dish too much. Some cooks, particularly from the old school, believe in "the more the merrier" method. The richness of floating fat on top of a serving dish indicates prosperity, generosity, and a will to please one's family and friends. So maybe it is this tradition that has contributed to the idea that Indian food is fattening.

It must be remembered, too, that ideas about reducing fat in the diet for it to be considered healthy are relatively recent. In the times of my mother's generation, for example, things like pure ghee, homemade butter, and whole milk were considered some of the top health foods and were used quite generously. Vegetable oils were then sneered at and thought of as cheap and nasty products, positively harmful to health.

Colorful shrines with offerings are found at every turning in India.

A change of attitude

Things have changed quite a bit since then. Cooking with vegetable oils is now more than acceptable in the Asian community and the emphasis on pure ghee and home-made butter has become almost a thing of the past. It must be remembered, however, that it is also healthier to use less of *any* fat rather than more.

Nutritional research indicates that it is not carbohydrates but excess fat that must be avoided if we are to be healthy. An awareness of the importance of reducing fat in our diet is gradually affecting what we choose to eat and what we avoid.

Properly prepared Indian food, where care has been taken to keep fat to the minimum, is very healthy and, according to one of the leading food manufacturers, tops the popularity chart. Also, a great many of the foods that nutritionists highly recommend for healthy living are included in Indian cuisine: pulses and grains, wholemeal flour, plain unsweetened yogurt, garlic, ginger, fresh fruit and vegetables, and lean meat, or no meat at all. The only dark cloud in an otherwise blue sky is the use of ghee or oils, but, if its use is reduced to the minimum, it will not cause difficulties.

*The Taj Mahal, Shah Jehan's mausoleum for his wife Mumtaz Mahul, is synonymous
with the romance and grandeur of Indian history.*

I know from experience that the natural tendency when cooking a curry is to add (and keep on adding) oil until you have enough in the pan for the onions and spices to cook with great ease. However, all you have to do for healthier eating is resist this inclination and add no more than is absolutely necessary. During the cooking process oil becomes trapped in or hidden by the onions and spices, giving the false impression that there is hardly any, but just carry on cooking over a low heat, stirring from time to time, and be patient – it will make it eventually appear!

A good thing to do is to keep on decreasing the quantity of oil each time you cook so you develop an awareness, and the habit, of using only an absolutely essential amount.

Cooking in an excessive amount of oil has just become a habit for most Indian cooks. We don't feel comfortable if the onions and spices are not well surrounded by it. It feels as if the presence of oil in quantity is going to make our job easy and, to some extent, it does. As you will have noticed, it certainly prevents the onions sticking to the pan and it

also helps to turn them a rich, golden color in half the time (or so it seems); we feel sure that the little pool of bubbling oil around the masala paste is going to "cook it better" for us! It is this false feeling of comfort and confidence that we must shake off to move in the right direction.

Overcooking vegetables, draining away the goodness and, finally, serving the remains with huge dollops of butter, in an effort to rejuvenate the lifeless vegetables is equally detrimental to healthy eating. Even in these enlightened times, potatoes, if not deep-fried as French fries, are roasted in a pool of oil to increase their taste and crispiness; sauces and gravies are quite often made from cream, butter, and other animal fats; meat still comes with a thick rind of fat. A good curry starts with the leanest meat and the freshest vegetables, so all we have to do is limit the oil we add.

The main thing is that to eat healthily, whatever the cuisine, it is necessary to first have an awareness of *what* we need to eat to be healthy and then work to follow the guidelines in the way the food is prepared.

Fresh, healthy dishes sold on Indian streets.

The lowfat diet ideal, applied to all the food and to any particular cuisine, offers us great advantages. It ensures good health and excess weight loss without even trying, which has to be good news!

A 22-week study undertaken at Cornell University, found that people lost weight without being on a diet simply by eating lowfat foods. The women who took part in the study followed a diet that provided just 25 percent of calories from fat, compared to the average contribution of 33 percent in the American diet. Another interesting finding of the study was that in a traditional slimming diet carbohydrate intake is cut to reduce calories and this slows down the body's metabolism of fats, which is counter-productive. Lowfat food, however, does not affect the metabolic rate like this. David Levitsky, Professor of Nutrition and Psychology at the university, said, "With lowfat diets, we don't see any metabolism changes. We suspect that metabolism regulatory mechanisms are related to carbohydrate consumption, not fat."

It was found, too, that the women who followed the low-fat diet did not suffer any of the usual side-effects of dieting, like food cravings or depression, that, in the end, make it harder to stick to a diet, especially once they have reached a plateau of weight loss. Professor Levitsky said, "Our studies confirm that people can lose weight without dieting. The weight loss is slow but persistent and should result in a 10 percent loss of bodyweight per year."

The results, published in the May 1991 issue of the *American Journal of Clinical Nutrition*, show that the women who ate lowfat foods lost weight steadily at the rate of about ½ pound a week, even though they were not counting calories or watching the amount of food they were consuming. It is believed that men should respond in the same way, too.

When I first started experimenting with lowfat cooking, I thought that a great deal of taste and flavor would be lost. In order to retain the true essence of Indian dishes, I stuck to the authentic recipe, but simply cut down the amount of fat I used as much as I could. I was delighted with the results – the food tasted, if not better, just as good. An added advantage was knowing that it was healthier to eat this way.

It is true, and I hate to admit it, that frying onions and spices in an adequate amount of oil does enhance the flavor of Indian food and, yes, it does make them easier to cook. However, there are ways to substitute whatever is lacking. Think of the ingredients that will increase the aroma and flavor – a few that come to my mind are ginger, garlic, fresh cilantro, roasted cumin and coriander seeds and, of course, my very special recipes for freshly ground garam masala. Slightly increasing the quantities of these herbs and spices and following a good recipe did the trick.

I strongly recommend that you keep a good set of measuring spoons handy and make sure to *always* measure the oil, increasing it only when you have to increase the quantity of food you are preparing because you are feeding more people. Just stick to this rule and you will reap the advantages.

A major part of my work is to pass on this knowledge and an awareness that Indian food can be cooked in a healthy, clean, honest way and still be enjoyed just as much, and that "oily" certainly does not mean "better" or "tastier" as some people tend to believe. Indian food is as popular as ever and we know that it is because it is so delicious, but we also now know that it can be healthy, if only we choose to make it so. Follow my recipes and you will see how.

A few words about Indian ingredients

Read the following sections for the best results when using the recipes in this book and for important information regarding methods and weights and measures. Also, there are some basic recipes here for ease of reference as you will need to refer to them frequently.

MEAT AND POULTRY

Meat, as we know, has a fairly high calorific value, which is mainly due to its saturated fat content. We, therefore, need to take care to choose only the leanest meat and trim away any visible fat before cooking it and, furthermore, eat it in moderation to reduce our consumption of fat as much as possible.

Dishes like Bhoona Gosht and the various kormas where meat is cooked on its own, should always be served with a generous amount of vegetable bhajis, lentils, and grains to balance the meal. The best thing to do is to add a fairly large quantity of vegetables to a small portion of lean meat. This has two advantages: It increases the quantity of the dish without adding very many calories or fat, making it healthy, economical, and convenient, as well as adding the flavor of the chosen vegetables. You can create a number of different dishes with their own very distinct flavors just by varying the vegetables slightly. Anyway, in an Indian or Pakistani home, a meat curry is seldom eaten on its own.

SOME USEFUL TIPS FOR MEAT AND POULTRY It has taken me a lifetime of experimentation to find this out, but I now know that the Punjabi way of preparing meat is the best. It is simple and straightforward, easy and economical and, best of all, it is the least fattening.

My mother, being from northern India and a city dweller, is proud of the rich and regal cuisine of that region, which has a strong Mogul influence. She was merely a teenager when, as a young bride, she moved from Lucknow, a most distinguished town, well-known for the sophistication of its Urdu language and its exotic cuisine, to the Punjab. Throughout her married life she has stuck to that particular style of cooking and, in fact, she was somewhat snobbish about the exotic and rich dishes that only she knew how to prepare in that remote village in the Punjab.

When the honeymoon period was over for her and she was allowed to take charge of the kitchen, she found her-self surrounded by the local women, expressing their amazement at her paper-thin chapatis and unique, aromatic dishes cooked in a totally un-Punjabi style. Everyone was extremely impressed and she secretly enjoyed the sense of power it gave her!

Punjabi food is simple and straightforward in comparison. People from that part of India drink a lot of salty lassi (lightly diluted yogurt drink) and sugarcane juice. Their diet mostly consists of unrefined grains and flours and they eat very little meat.

I knew about the Punjabi method of cooking meat and other dishes all along, but, for some reason, never put it into practice, not until I began searching for ways and means of creating lowfat foods. To my amazement, I realized that the solution had always been there, staring me in the face, and yet I had missed it!

This beautifully prepared meal is typical of food served in thalis.

PUNJABI STYLE OF COOKING MEAT Ordinarily the onions and spices are fried in oil at the initial stage of preparing most meat curries, followed by a sufficient amount of water added to the curry to let the meat cook. In Punjabi cooking, the order is reversed. You begin by adding water into the meat along with onions, ginger, garlic, and the rest of the spices and leave it to cook slowly, very much like stew.

The gravy, toward the end of the cooking period, appears to be slightly coated with an oily sheen by the fat released from the meat and bones. So when the time comes to add oil, one tends to use a lot less than otherwise. Best of all, it can be left out altogether in cooking this way, as in some of the recipes such as Daal Gosht and Kadoo Gosht. Each tablespoon of oil costs 120 calories so, if you decide to leave it out, you would be cutting down on calories quite considerably.

Some vegetables, like eggplants, okra, mushrooms and cauliflower, crave for oil and soak it up like a sponge – no matter how much you put in, it keeps on disappearing. You must be firm with yourself when cooking any of these and watch out for the temptation to add "just a bit more."

When buying lamb or beef you will find that either braising steak or meat from the leg or shoulder will be the leanest. Even so, trim any visible fat off before using.

Traditionally, boneless meat is seldom used in Indian cooking. Indeed, bones are included with the meat because they add flavor to the sauce, and we all know that the meat nearest the bone is the sweetest.

With ground meat, to ensure that you are buying the best quality and leanest meat, choose a lean piece of meat and grind it yourself in a food processor.

The best thing about Indian chicken dishes is that it is never cooked with the skin on. As the skin is where the majority of the fat is, this helps a great deal to minimize the presence of saturated fats.

FISH AND SHRIMP DISHES
Apart from the coastal areas in India and Pakistan, eating fish is still not part of the normal diet, and for most people it is something they generally do without.

Yet seafood is delicious cooked in the Indian style, which is mostly fried, steamed, curried, or barbecued. River or freshwater fish is quite sought-after and people travel a great distance to the exclusive places where it can be bought.

When buying fish, make sure that it feels firm and looks plump and not flabby. Pay special attention to the eyes; they must be bright and alert, not dull and cloudy. It is best to buy the fish on the day you intend cooking it.

Sunset in Cochin – a haven not only for sailors, but also for seafood gourmets.

This colorful display gives an indication of the enormous variety of fresh produce available in India.

VEGETABLES

Back home, the Indian housewife is a bit spoilt when it comes to buying fruit and vegetables. It is generally accepted that it is her right to pick, probe, smell, and squeeze any number of fruits and vegetables she likes while selecting the very best ones for her own basket. That's the way my mother shopped, so she was rather shocked when she was not allowed to do so in my local markets in England. However, there are more Asian stores now, where it is understood that the shopper wants to choose the fruit and vegetables bought – and even haggle over the price – and supermarkets have increased their ranges of fruit and vegetables and other ingredients used in Indian cuisine and there, too, you can pick what you want yourself, so things have improved enormously.

My mother's years of experience of examining fruits and vegetables at close range have turned her into an expert buyer. She can sort out the best from the rest at a single glance or by touching them. I have learned a lot from her and pass on some of her best tips here so you know what to look for, too.

SOME USEFUL TIPS FOR CHOOSING VEGETABLES "You have to be extra careful with some vegetables," my mother would say, hoping her grown-up daughters were taking it in. Take okra, for instance, the pods should be crisp and fresh enough to snap when you apply just slight pressure. For eggplants she would say that they've "got to be a combination of velvet and marble" – soft and silky to the touch, but, when you tighten your grip a bit, it should feel firm and must spring back immediately no matter how hard the pressure. It must never feel spongy, hollow, or dented.

"What about chilies and peppers?" we would ask. "Definitely cool and crisp and shimmering, almost like a mirror, so you can see your reflection in them . . . no good when they are turning red due to staleness and go coarse, wrinkly and limp," she would reply.

For cauliflower she would say, "Well, it should be so tight and firmly held together that even a drop of water would not be able to seep through it! The best ones are like a huge white flower and the green leaves and stems surround the vegetable like an alert army of guards. It should be cooked unhurriedly, strictly in its own moisture, never

Vegetables come just as fresh as you want them.

touch it with water except when you wash it, never. Of course, the cauliflower is at its best when just slightly underdone, every floweret separate and firm, ready to be counted. They should be like a superb arrangement of flowers in your serving dish."

SEEDING GREEN CHILIES The worst thing about chilies is the fear that they will make a dish too hot. I believe you either use a small amount of green chilies or you don't use them at all. Seeding them does not make much sense to me: It is a really tedious job and, in my opinion, a waste of time and energy, so I have never understood why all the cookbooks recommend it. The seeds are the hottest part of the chili, but most recipes call for a small number of chilies or, often, just one. Most Asian households do not remove them and I have certainly never had any complaints from non-Asian friends, so be daring and at least try it and see!

If, after all, you do wish to take the seeds out, cut the chili open under running water and rinse it out.

When chopping chilies, do not rub your eyes afterward as the seeds will have some of the oil on them, so wash your hands well after handling chilies.

PULSES

Called daals in India, there are a great many more varieties than the humble red lentil and few beans that have generally been the only ones used in any quantity in the West. With the spread of vegetarianism in more recent years, however, many of them can now be bought from supermarkets, but for an even wider range, try an Asian grocer's. They are available either whole or split, are high in fiber, low in fat,

and extremely tasty, so try some of the recipes that use them and reap the benefits.

Channa daal are rather like split peas but are a little bit smaller and a lovely yellow color.

Chick-peas are readily available either dried or ready-cooked in cans. They are a beige color and round with a wrinkled appearance. Chick-pea flour is used a great deal in Indian cuisine but can be a little difficult to find except in Indian grocer's stores.

Black-eyed peas – called lobia in India – are popular in Southern cooking and easier to find.

Kidney beans release a toxic substance while they are being cooked, but, as long as you boil them rapidly for at least 10 minutes at the beginning of the cooking time, this substance is destroyed completely.

If you are at all worried, just use the canned ones, substituting a 14-ounce can for every 3 cups of dried beans required by the recipe.

Moong daal are the split mung beans that are used to produce beansprouts.

Split red lentils, or masoor daal in India, are the commonest lentil and can be found everywhere. They are easy to cook and are transformed in Indian dishes into something really special – a far cry from a random addition to a winter stew. The less common whole, unsplit version is also used in Indian cooking.

Garlic – the very soul of almost all Indian dishes.

In Praise of Basmati Rice

Nature has blessed basmati rice with the quality of being able to reach its peak of perfection with minimal external help and this puts it in a class of its own. You have to pay a little more for it than other rice, but the end result makes it worth every penny. Not only is it so much easier to cook, its unique taste and flavor add a special touch to the whole meal.

In the West a lot of people still think that the route to perfect rice is one only a few can travel and it definitely is not them. If you are one of these people, then try basmati rice. Take the example of my daughter. Being an ardent student, she is not too keen on cooking just now, but has good intentions to learn everything properly one day. However, since the age of 12, she has been able to cook rice without any difficulty. If she can do it, anybody can – as long as it is basmati rice, that is.

You will have noticed while washing or rinsing most brands of white rice that the water becomes milky. It is this substance that causes all the problems: It thickens into a gluey liquid during cooking, making the rice grains cling together. With basmati rice, on the other hand, the water starts to run clear after the first couple of rinses and, anyway, what milkiness there is is not substantial. This lack of gluten means that the rice grains stay separate, even after they have been thoroughly cooked.

Some useful tips for cooking rice The two simple secrets of cooking most types of rice are, first, cooking it in exactly the right amount of water and, second, providing the right amounts of heat at the right time.

Measure the cooking water according to the volume of rice to be cooked. Measuring with a tea cup makes this very simple. The rule is, 1½ cups of water for each cup of rice. Remember this simple technique and you won't go wrong. It is as simple as that.

It is a good idea, too, if you have the time, to soak the rice for at least 10 to 15 minutes in water for the best results.

We have another very useful and clever technique in the East for checking that we have added the right amount of water. Add the water to the rice in a medium-sized saucepan, swirl it around a bit to level the rice, then dip your middle finger into the center of the pan. For a small quantity of rice, such as is mostly used in this book, the tip of your finger should touch the bottom of the pan and the water level reach the first knuckle of your finger. Add or remove water as necessary. This method never fails and takes only a few seconds to check.

If you are cooking larger quantities of rice, you change the technique slightly – the tip of your middle finger should rest on the surface of the rice, not on the bottom of the pan.

This simple and pretty accurate method has been widely practiced in India and Pakistan as long as anyone can remember, passed on from generation to generation.

Another important point to remember is to use a heavy-bottomed pan when cooking rice because a light, thin-based pan will easily burn the rice in the last stage of cooking when almost all the water has been absorbed.

Some basic recipes

Chapatis

The chapati is bread at its simplest. The ingredients are just flour and water – no butter, oil or seasoning, not even salt – yet, by bringing these two simple, basic ingredients together, you can create one of the most popular breads eaten in India and Pakistan.

The most common Indian bread – chapati – is simply baked; here, on the inner lining of an oven. Hence the term tandoori roti.

Lowfat chapatis

There are some Indian dishes that can only be enjoyed with a chapati or some other kind of bread – Cabbage and Carrot Bhaji (see page 66), smoked eggplants and some potato dishes, such as Phalli Aloo (see page 64), Aloo ka Bhurta (see page 70), and other dishes like these that are too dry to serve with rice. Poori, paratha, or naan taste very good with these dishes, too. Lightly toasted sliced bread can also be served with most curries or bhajis. Some dry curries and mostly all sorts of bhajis and lentil dishes make excellent toppings for sliced bread, which is often eaten in place of chapatis.

Of all the Indian breads, chapatis contain the fewest calories. Some people like to add a couple of tablespoons of oil to the flour when preparing the dough, but there is no need to do so. It just adds calories unnecessarily.

The best part is that you can make a batch of dough, keep it in the refrigerator, decide how many calories you can

afford to allocate for the bread part of your meal and weigh out an appropriate amount of dough before you cook it (or them). It is easy to work out the calories for the chosen amount of dough – each ounce of dough consists of 60 calories. You can see that you are in total control here – your chapatis will have as many calories as you want them to have, no more, no less.

Thanks to that wonderful invention, the microwave, a cold, even stale, chapati can be brought back to life within half a minute. Chapatis may also be frozen and rejuvenated by placing them in a microwave for less than a minute.

If heating defrosted chapatis under a broiler to reheat them, dampen them slightly and cook them for half a minute on each side. Wrap them in a cloth and use immediately.

Chapati dough can also be frozen and defrosted when required. Otherwise the dough may be kept in the refrigerator in a covered container for 2–3 days. If you notice that, toward the end of this period, it has gone slightly softer or runny, add a little flour and knead it again for a few minutes to make it as firm and pliable as you like.

It usually takes a little while to get the hang of making good chapatis, but once you master the skill, you will be rewarded with delicious bread in a matter of minutes. Besides, the learning part is such fun, like trying to toss your very first crêpe. Naturally, while you are learning to make them, your chapatis will be all sorts of shapes and sizes, but don't be disappointed if some of them come out of the pan looking like Humpty Dumpty with several dangling legs because, no matter how much you go wrong with the shape, they will still taste good.

All you need is a little perseverance and you will soon be creating chapatis with a soft silky texture that are perfectly round.

You will need 1½ cups of wholemeal flour, ½ cup all-purpose flour, and ¾ cup of water.

Total Calories: 800 (including the flour for dredging) – will make 6 chapatis weighing 3 ounces each, costing 180 calories per chapati.*

*60 calories to 1 ounce of dough.

Mix a little water at a time into the flour in a mixing bowl. When all the water has been incorporated, start kneading the dough, moistening your hands frequently to ease it off the bowl. Soon it will feel soft and pliable, very much like any other bread dough.

Cover the bowl with a damp cloth and let it stand for at least 30 minutes.

If you think the dough feels too soft and sticky, you can change its texture. Roll the dough onto a floured surface and knead it until it feels firm and is easy to handle – neither wet nor dry (the tendency will be to make the dough firm, but you must remember that if the dough is too firm, the chapatis will turn out crispy and a bit cookie-like).

Heat a fairly large, thick-bottomed skillet if you do not have an Indian iron griddle, called a tava, that is used for this purpose. Set it over a fairly high heat to warm it up, then reduce the heat.

Break off a small piece of dough (2–3 ounces), roll it into a ball in your palm, then roll it out on a floured surface in the following way. Start rolling it out gently and *lightly* until you have made a thick, round disk. Be really light-handed at this stage as I know from experience that if you press the dough a bit too hard it becomes pasted to the surface. If this does happen, do not worry, just scrape it off completely and start again, remembering to roll it out with feather-light strokes and make sure you keep the weight of the rolling pin itself off the chapati dough, resting it mostly between your fingers and thumbs. You might find it necessary to re-dust the surface several times with flour to stop the dough sticking to it, but be careful not to use more than

is really necessary, otherwise the dry flour clinging to the chapati will start burning when you cook it, causing the chapati to discolor and a lot of smoke to rise.

Carefully place the rolled out chapati in the hot pan, keeping the heat to medium. You will see that, within a few seconds, a shadowed look will start to spread beneath the chapati. *Immediately* these shadows appear, carefully lift the chapati up by its edge and turn it over. Now watch out for tiny bubbles to form on the surface of the chapati after about 30 seconds. As soon as they appear, lift and turn it over again, for the last time. (It is important not to turn the chapati over too many times as it will ruin the texture, making it hard and leathery.)

With a clean dishtowel, press the chapati down, especially at the edges, to ensure that it cooks evenly. This will make the chapati puff up slightly and golden spots will appear on the surface, indicating that the chapati is cooked. (If the heat is right and you get into a rhythm, it should not take more than a minute to cook each chapati.) Wrap them up in a dishtowel as soon as they are ready, to keep them warm and soft, and eat them straight away as they are at their best when just cooked.

Flour and water being mixed to make chapatis in a family home.

TAMARIND PULP

Tamarind pods are similar in shape and size to a large fava bean, only they are brown in color, with hard, woody shells around the pulp in the center. They grow on tall trees and, once peeled, are seeded and pressed into thick blocks or slabs and dried.

The pulp has a special sour taste that contributes a pleasant tartness to the food or sauces it is added to.

Here is how to make up Tamarind Pulp from dried tamarind:

Break a walnut-sized (about 2-ounce) piece of tamarind from a block of dried tamarind pulp and soak it in ⅔ cup of hot water for an hour or so.

Mash the pulp by rubbing it with your fingers, then push it through a strainer over a bowl and squeeze what remains well to extract the maximum amount of juice from it. Discard the stringy fibrous bits of tamarind that remain in the strainer. The Tamarind Pulp you now have in the bowl will keep in the refrigerator for a little over a week or you can freeze it in an ice-cube tray so that the frozen cubes can easily be added to a dish as and when the recipe calls for it.

TAMARIND SAUCE

The following is a basic Tamarind Sauce recipe, which has an intriguing sweet-and-sour taste. You can easily turn it into more of a fruit chutney by adding pineapple rings, banana slices, and pitted and sliced prunes. Grated carrots can be added, too.

It will keep for over a week in the refrigerator, but if you are making some quite a bit in advance of when you will use it, freeze it in small amounts or ice-cube trays.

You will need ⅔ cup of Tamarind Pulp (see the recipe left), ½ teaspoon Roasted and Crushed Cumin Seeds (see page 17), 4–5 teaspoons artificial sugar, a pinch of Garam Masala (see page 18; optional), a pinch of chili powder, ¼ teaspoon salt and 1 tablespoon of lemon juice.

Dilute the pulp in a saucepan by adding about ½ cup of water, then add the Cumin Seeds, sugar, Garam Masala, if using, chili powder, and salt. Bring it to a boil and simmer for a few minutes. Add the lemon juice, then taste the sauce and adjust the seasoning to your liking. When it is ready, leave it to cool. Serve it chilled.

Tamarind Sauce.

Ginger and Garlic Paste.

GINGER AND GARLIC PASTE

This Ginger and Garlic Paste is very useful and will keep for 2 to 3 weeks in an airtight jar in the refrigerator.

It freezes well, too, and there are various ways in which to do this. If you cook Indian food only once in awhile, then freezing the Ginger and Garlic Paste in separate, small quantities is the best. Do not keep it in the refrigerator for longer than 3 weeks or make the mistake of freezing all of it in one container. Instead, either freeze it in an ice-cube tray reserved for this purpose (as it will impart its flavor to the tray) or spread the paste onto a cookie sheet and, once frozen, remove the slab, breaking it into pieces, and keep it wrapped up in a plastic bag.

Alternatively, cut squares of foil and put 2 teaspoonfuls onto each piece and wrap them to make several tiny packages and put these into a plastic container or bag and freeze.

Whichever method you choose, you prepare yourself for months ahead and cooking Indian food becomes so much simpler and you can prepare wonderful dishes whenever you want without having to store on a special trip, which kills the spontaneity of it all.

Making it is simplicity itself – here is what you do:

You will need 4 ounces of fresh ginger root, lightly scraped, washed and cut into chunks, and the same amount of fresh garlic, peeled.

Put the ingredients into a blender with a very little water, just sufficient to facilitate the grinding process.

Spoon the paste into an airtight jar and store it on the bottom shelf in the refrigerator or freeze it (see above). Total calories: 72.

ROASTED AND CRUSHED CUMIN SEEDS

The toasting and crushing of cumin seeds always reminds me of the story of the genie being released from the bottle. The big, bold aroma rushing out of those tiny seeds is just as amazing and powerful to me as the magical genie in the story.

These seeds are termed white cumin seeds and are widely used in Indian cuisine. The seeds are, in fact, brownish in color, not white at all, but they are known as white cumin to differentiate them from the other variety, black cumin, which is almost black. The term Shahi Zeera is also often used for black cumin. It is important to note that black cumin seeds cannot be substituted for the ordinary white cumin seeds. Also, *never* use horticultural seeds in cooking; always buy them from an Asian grocer's or look in the herbs section of other stores.

For Roasted and Crushed Cumin Seeds you will need 2 ounces of white cumin seeds.

Heat a heavy-bottomed skillet over a medium heat. When it is hot, reduce the heat and drop the cumin seeds into it. Stir them immediately and continuously with a wooden spoon.

In another couple of minutes, the cumin seeds will turn slightly pinkish brown in color. When they do, switch off the heat, shake, and remove the pan from the stove and leave the seeds to cool.

Once they have cooled, pour them into a blender and grind them for half a second. Alternatively, pour them into a plastic bag and crush them with a rolling pin. The seeds become crispy during the roasting process and so they break easily – only a little pressure is needed to crush them.

Put the Roasted and Crushed Cumin Seeds into an airtight jar immediately and keep it in a cool, dry place.

Roasted and Crushed Cumin Seeds.

ROASTED AND CRUSHED CORIANDER SEEDS

As with cumin seeds, never use horticultural coriander seeds in cooking; always either buy them from Asian grocers or look in the herbs section of other stores.

Coriander seeds can be roasted and crushed in exactly the same way as cumin seeds.

For ground coriander, grind the seeds until they turn into a fine powder. For either kind, storing in an airtight jar is very important if you are not to lose that delicious nutty aroma.

Garam Masala.

GARAM MASALA

Here is a recipe for a basic garam masala that is invaluable for all kinds of everyday recipes, but you may vary the proportions to satisfy your own tastes once you have tried it.

You will need 2 ounces black cardamom pods, 1-ounce piece of cinnamon stick, 1 ounce of cloves, and 2 ounces of peppercorns.

Heat a large, heavy-bottomed skillet and, when it is hot, reduce the heat and add the black cardamom pods and cinnamon stick. With a wooden spoon, move the cardamom and cinnamon around constantly for 2 minutes.

Add the cloves and peppercorns and carry on shuffling the spices around for another 1 minute. Switch off the heat, but still keep on stirring until the skillet eventually loses its heat and then leave to cool completely.

Pour the roasted spices into a blender or coffee grinder and grind until you have a fine powder. (If the Garam Masala appears coarse and stringy because of the cardamom shells, strain it and discard what will not pass through the strainer). Store it in an airtight bottle or jar.

GARNISHING GARAM MASALA

Combine 2 tablespoons Roasted and Crushed Cumin Seeds (see page 17) and 2 tablespoons Roasted Coriander Seeds (see left). Grind them for a second in an electric blender or coffee grinder until you have a fine powder. Add 1 tablespoon of Garam Masala (see left) to it and grind for another second to blend the mixture thoroughly. Store it in an airtight bottle or jar.

GREEN GARLIC SAUCE

In an electric blender combine 1 small green bell pepper cut into small pieces, 4 cloves of garlic, 2 whole green chilies (or ¼ teaspoon chili powder), 3–4 tablespoons lemon juice, 1 teaspoon sugar, 4 tablespoons chopped cilantro leaves, ¼–½ teaspoon salt and 2–3 tablespoons water. Chill before using.

DRY WHOLE CHILIES These are used vastly in Indian cooking and can be used whole or broken or even crushed. It's safer to use them whole, especially if you are not used to very hot food, and you can always discard them just before serving the dish, if you are afraid you might chew on them accidentally. Chili powder can be substituted, but dry whole chilies have a subtle flavor of their own that you will grow to find indispensable.

Food values

Note that the calories boxes at the end of each recipe give the total calories for that dish and those per portion, but do not include those for chapatis or rice or other accompaniments so that you have the flexibility to serve whatever you want with each dish depending on how much of your calorie allowance you have used up.

Dry whole chilies, found in abundance throughout India.

Spicy Meatloaf with Tamarind Sauce

Kofta Sticks

Chick-peas in Yogurt Sauce

Mixed Vegetable Bhajias

Spicy Potato Patties

Appetizers

Fish in Silver Packages

Crunchy Vegetable Kabobs

Dry Masala Kidney Beans

Spicy Meatloaf with Tamarind Sauce

SERVES 4

INGREDIENTS

¼ *pound onions, roughly chopped*

2 tsp grated fresh ginger root

2 green chilies

1 tbsp lowfat plain yogurt

2–3 plump cloves garlic

3 tbsp chopped cilantro leaves

½ pound ground lean lamb or beef

1 tbsp cornstarch

½ tsp chili powder

¼ tsp Garam Masala (see page 18)

small pinch ground mace

2 tsp lemon juice

FOOD VALUE

	TOTAL	PER PORTION (¼)
TOTAL FAT	11.2 g	2.8 g
SATURATED FAT	4.6 g	1.1 g
CHOLESTEROL	135 mg	34 mg
ENERGY (calories)	447	112

This is an excellent party dish because it can be prepared beforehand, chilled a day or two ahead or frozen for a longer period in advance of the party and then simply defrosted and served cold or heated in an oven or microwave on the day. To keep it moist and fragrant, it should be covered with a few fried onions or raw onion rings soaked in lemon juice, sliced tomatoes, fresh mint and cilantro leaves. Serve thin slices with onion rings, cucumber and carrot sticks, wedges of lemon and, best of all, Tamarind Sauce (see page 16).

METHOD

1 Put the onion, ginger, green chilies, yogurt, garlic and cilantro leaves in an electric blender and blend. Pour the paste into a small bowl.

2 Put the ground meat into a medium-sized bowl, add the paste together with the remaining ingredients, except the lemon juice.

3 Mix the meat thoroughly, kneading it for a couple of minutes to ensure that the herbs and spices are evenly and well distributed.

4 With moistened hands, press the mixture into a round or oblong loaf shape, ensuring an uncracked, smooth surface.

5 Place the loaf in the middle of a piece of foil large enough to cover it loosely and let it stand for 20 to 30 minutes before baking. Preheat the oven to 425°F.

6 Place the wrapped loaf on a cookie tray and bake it in the preheated oven for 20 minutes. Unfold the foil to reveal the top of the loaf and bake it for another 5 to 7 minutes, until it is golden brown.

VARIATION
Kofta Sticks
SERVES 4

Form the ground meat mixture as for the Spicy Meatloaf into Kofta shapes (small, round balls) and cook them under a hot broiler for 7 to 8 minutes, turning them regularly so they cook evenly. Drain them on paper towels.

Put the koftas onto toothpicks and serve them on a platter, surrounded by a crispy salad and lemon wedges.

A tablespoon of Green Garlic Sauce (see page 18) mixed into Scallion and Cucumber Raita (see page 114) makes a lovely dip for the koftas and, of course, Tamarind Sauce (see page 16) with grated carrots is an absolute must.

DAHI CHANNA CHAAT
Chick-peas in Yogurt Sauce
SERVES 4

INGREDIENTS

1 cup lowfat plain yogurt
3 oz red and green bell peppers
¾ cup chopped cucumber
2 scallions, chopped
1½ cups canned chick-peas, drained
½ tsp chili powder
1 clove garlic
½ tsp cumin seeds, crushed
1 tsp artificial sugar
salt and pepper to taste
1 tsp dried mint
2 tbsp cilantro leaves or fresh mint or chives, chopped

FOOD VALUE

	TOTAL	PER PORTION (¼)
TOTAL FAT	8.6 g	2.2 g
SATURATED FAT	1.7 g	0.4 g
CHOLESTEROL	8 mg	2 mg
ENERGY (calories)	398	100

This dish makes a lovely appetizer for a summer meal, and it is popular at parties, too. Poured over a baked potato it makes a substantial meal.

METHOD
1. Beat ⅔ cup of water into the yogurt to dilute it.
2. Wash, dry, and chop the peppers.
3. Pour the chick-peas into the yogurt. Add the chili powder, garlic, cumin seeds, sugar, and salt and pepper and mix thoroughly. Add the vegetables and mint and mix again. Garnish with chopped cilantro, mint or chives and chill well before serving.

Mixed Vegetable Bhajias

SERVES 4

INGREDIENTS

½ cup chick-pea flour

a pinch of baking powder

¼ tsp chili powder

a pinch of turmeric

½ tsp cumin seeds, crushed

½ tsp coriander seeds, crushed

1–2 tbsp cilantro leaves, chopped
(optional)

½ tsp salt

1 ounce zucchini

1 ounce eggplant

2 ounces onion

2 tbsp oil

FOOD VALUE

	TOTAL	PER PORTION (¼)
TOTAL FAT	25.1 g	6.28 g
SATURATED FAT	2.85 g	0.71 g
CHOLESTEROL	0	0
ENERGY (calories)	388	97

What, bhajias (or Pakoras as they are called in Pakistan) on a lowfat menu? I, too, would have thought it impossible as bhajias are always deep-fried and, as a result, loaded with calories. As they are one of the most delicious savory snacks in the world, though I just had to work out a receipe for bhajias that would be suitably low in fat, and I have done it. These are not as crispy and light in texture as they would have been had they been deep-fried, but, even so, the combination of these spicy bhajias and tangy Tamarind Sauce (see page 16) still tastes heavenly and can be eaten with a clear conscience.

I use chick-pea flour (basen) for the batter but you can also try cornstarch, but the results will not be quite as good.

METHOD

1 Sift the chick-pea flour and baking powder into a small mixing bowl. Add the chili powder, turmeric, cumin and coriander seeds, if using, cilantro leaves, if using, and salt. Add about ⅓ cup of water and mix it well, making a smooth batter. Let it stand for 15 minutes.

2 Wash, dry, and slice the zucchini and eggplants finely. Slice the onion finely, too. Just before you are ready to cook, add these vegetables to the chick-pea batter, coating them well.

3 Heat half the oil in a medium-sized nonstick skillet, then spoon the battered vegetables into it. Reduce the heat to medium and cook for about 1 minute. Turn them over and cook for another minute or so, shaking the pan frequently.

5 Try to get them as crispy as you possibly can in that limited amount of oil. Remove and drain on paper towels. Repeat using the second tablespoon of oil and serve these hot.

ALOO KI TIKYA
Spicy Potato Patties
SERVES 4

INGREDIENTS

14 ounces potatoes
1 tbsp lemon juice
1 tbsp fresh mint, chopped, or unsweetened mint sauce
1/2 tsp salt
1 small onion, finely chopped
2 tsp coriander seeds, crushed
1 tsp cumin seeds
1/4 tsp chili powder
2 green chilies, finely chopped
3 tbsp chopped cilantro
1 large egg
2 tsp oil

FOOD VALUE

	TOTAL	PER PORTION (1/4)
TOTAL FAT	11.7 g	2.9 g
SATURATED FAT	2.2 g	0.6 g
CHOLESTEROL	181 mg	45 mg
ENERGY (calories)	438	110

Potatoes have a natural affinity with the herbs and spices and are especially receptive to the cumin, fresh cilantro and green chili of this recipe.

The tikyas (burgers) freeze well so they can be microwaved whenever needed. They go well with Tamarind Sauce (see page 16).

METHOD

1 Peel and chop the potatoes, then boil them until they are tender.

2 Meanwhile, mix the lemon juice, mint or mint sauce and a pinch of salt into the onion. Set this mixture for filling the patties to one side.

3 Break the potatoes and mash them lightly so the mixture is still slightly lumpy. Add the coriander and cumin seeds, chili powder, green chilies, cilantro leaves, and salt. Blend these herbs and spices well into the mashed potatoes.

4 Divide the potato mixture into 8 equal portions. Dampen your hands a little and roll each portion in your palm. Make a dent in the ball you've made, fill it with a tiny amount of the mint and onion filling, cover the filling, and flatten each ball gently to form a burger shape.

5 Just before frying these patties, beat the egg and season it lightly. Heat a large, nonstick skillet and grease it with half the oil. When the pan is fairly hot, dip each potato tikya into the egg and put it in the pan. Put the first 4 tikyas in the pan to sizzle for a minute or so, then turn them over and cook the other side until they are crispy and golden brown. Cook the remaining 4 tikyas in the same way.

Fish in Silver Packages

SERVES 1

INGREDIENTS

5 oz cod or haddock fillet
2 tsp lemon juice
salt to taste
1 tbsp cilantro leaves
1 fat clove garlic
1 green chili
1 tsp shredded coconut
¼ tsp sugar
2 tsp lowfat plain yogurt

FOOD VALUE

	TOTAL	PER PORTION
TOTAL FAT		4.1 g
SATURATED FAT		2.9 g
CHOLESTEROL		59 mg
ENERGY (calories)		137

The inspiration for this recipe is a well-known, festive Parsee dish known as Patra ni Macchi. The word "patra" means leaf and is used here because the fish pieces are first marinated, then wrapped in banana leaves before steaming, which results in fish that is moist and succulent.

The original recipe includes a very generous quantity of fresh coconut, which is unfortunate as the calories contained in that one ingredient are greater than the rest of the meal! Without it, though, this dish is very low in calories. Still, perhaps you could add just a hint of the traditional nutty flavor by adding a small quantity in the green masala paste rather than leave it out completely.

METHOD

1 Marinate the fish in the lemon juice and season lightly. Leave it to marinate for 15 to 20 minutes.

2 Grind the cilantro leaves, garlic, chili and coconut in a blender until the mixture forms a paste, then add the sugar, yogurt, and a pinch of salt, and mix them in thoroughly.

3 Smother the fish with this green masala paste on both sides. Wrap the fish loosely in foil and leave to marinate for at least 1 hour in the refrigerator. During that time, preheat the oven to 400°F.

4 Place the foil package on a cookie sheet and bake it in the preheated oven for about 15 minutes, or until it is just cooked through. Serve with a salad, and Tamarind Sauce (page 16).

Crunchy Vegetable Kabobs

SERVES 4

INGREDIENTS

6 oz cauliflower
3 oz cabbage
3 oz carrots
2 oz scallions or onion
6 oz potatoes, boiled
1 tbsp sunflower seeds
1 green chili, chopped
2–3 cloves garlic, chopped
1 tsp grated ginger root
½ tsp chili powder
½–1 tsp salt
½ tsp cumin seeds, crushed
freshly ground black pepper to taste
3 tbsp cilantro leaves, chopped
1 tbsp lemon juice
1 tbsp oil
1 large egg, beaten

FOOD VALUE

	TOTAL	PER PORTION (⅛)
TOTAL FAT	25.7 g	3.2 g
SATURATED FAT	4.1 g	0.5 g
CHOLESTEROL	181 mg	23 mg
ENERGY (calories)	496	62

Kabobs in Indian cooking are burger shapes with or without a filling rather than chunks of meat, fish, or vegetables strung on sticks and grilled. Spicy and delicious, they are very good to have in the freezer for snacks, appetizers, or main meals.

These crunchy kabobs, together with Tamarind Sauce (see page 16) and Green Garlic Sauce (see page 18) taste like a "piece of heaven," as my daughter would put it!

METHOD

1 Grate the cauliflower, cabbage, and carrots.

2 Chop the onions quite finely.

3 Mash the potatoes.

4 Toast the sunflower seeds, then set them to one side.

5 Combine the grated vegetables with the scallions or onion, mashed potatoes, green chili, garlic, and ginger.

6 Add the chili powder, salt, cumin seeds, freshly ground black pepper, cilantro leaves, and lemon juice. Mix the herbs, spices, and vegetables together thoroughly. Then mix in the sunflower seeds.

7 Divide the mixture into 8 equal portions and make burger shapes. Keep the kabobs in the refrigerator for 1 hour or so to firm up.

8 Grease a large, nonstick skillet with half the oil. Dip the first 4 kabobs into the egg and fry them gently over a medium heat. Turn them once, cooking both sides until they are crispy and golden brown. Use the remaining oil to cook the second batch of kabobs.

Gathering in the nets on Kovalam beach. The simple restaurants along what is often called India's finest beach offer a range of excellent seafood.

MASALA RAJMA
Dry Masala Kidney Beans
SERVES 4

See the information about cooking kidney beans on page 12 before starting this recipe.

INGREDIENTS

¾ cup dried red kidney beans

2 tsp Ginger and Garlic Paste (see page 17)

1 green chili, chopped

½ tsp chili powder

½ tsp salt

¼ tsp turmeric

¼ tsp Garam Masala (see page 18)

¼ tsp cumin seeds, crushed

2 tbsp finely chopped cilantro or mint leaves

1 tbsp lemon juice

FOOD VALUE

	TOTAL	PER PORTION (¼)
TOTAL FAT	1.8 g	0.5 g
SATURATED FAT	0.25 g	0.06 g
CHOLESTEROL	0	0
ENERGY (calories)	266	66

Red kidney beans are cooked here with spices until all the moisture has evaporated away and they are soft, and filled with aromatic juices.

You can substitute these for calorie-laden roasted peanuts at parties and a handful of these scattered over a crispy salad, not only adds to the color, but also provides a tasty, nutritious meal. Add them to any of the raitas and these pretty red beans, almost drowning in a pool of cool yogurt, make an easy meal that is a very enjoyable change.

METHOD

1 Soak the kidney beans for 3 to 4 hours in a medium-sized saucepan. Drain them well, then pour in 2½ cups of water.

2 Add all the ingredients except the cilantro or mint leaves, cumin seeds, and lemon juice. Cook over a high heat for the first 25 to 30 minutes, then reduce the heat and simmer for the next 35 to 40 minutes, reduce the heat and simmer for the next 35 to 40 minutes, or until the beans are tender but not broken or mushy.

3 Remove the lid and cook until all the moisture evaporates and the beans are soft but dry, taking care to ensure that they do not burn or stick to the pan.

4 Mix in the cumin seeds, cilantro or mint leaves, and lemon juice. Shake the beans, when they have cooled, place them on a serving platter.

A Semidry Lamb or Beef Curry with Pepper

Lamb with Chunks of Squash

Beef with Carrots and Peppers

Lamb with Lentils

Meat Dishes

Lamb with Okra and Onions

Lamb with Eggplants

Ground Meat with Peas and Peppers

Ground Meat with Cauliflower

Lamb with Twice the Amount of Onions

Meatballs in Thick Gravy

Meatballs with Broccoli or Spinach

Lamb with Cauliflower

BHOONA GOSHT
A Semidry Lamb or Beef Curry with Peppers
SERVES 4

INGREDIENTS

¾ lb leg of lamb, boned

2 oz green bell pepper

½ cup chopped onion

1 tbsp Ginger and Garlic Paste
(see page 17)

½ tsp chili powder

¼ tsp turmeric

½ tsp Garam Masala (see page 18)

½–¾ tsp salt

2 tbsp oil

⅓ cup chopped tomatoes

chopped chives or scallions,
to garnish

FOOD VALUE

	TOTAL	PER PORTION (¼)
TOTAL FAT	53.4 g	13.3 g
SATURATED FAT	17.4 g	4.4 g
CHOLESTEROL	277 mg	69 mg
ENERGY (calories)	812	203

METHOD

1 Wash and cut the meat into 1-inch cubes.

2 Cut the green pepper into ½-inch squares.

3 Put the meat in a medium-sized heavy-bottomed saucepan. Add the onion, Ginger and Garlic Paste, chili powder, turmeric, Garam Masala, and salt. Pour in 1¼ cups water, stir then cover the pan and bring it to a boil. Reduce the heat and simmer for 30 to 35 minutes.

4 Remove the lid, turn up the heat, and stir continuously until the moisture evaporates and the masala paste thickens. Then add the oil, stir it in and cook for another minute or so. This is a crucial time for the dish: the spices and oil must marry up well with the meat. Fry the mixture, adding a tiny amount of water, until the masala paste turns a slightly darker shade and begins to appear slightly glazed (this will take a couple of minutes).

5 Add the peppers and tomato, mix in well, and cook for 2 to 3 minutes.

6 Let the Bhoona Gosht stand for 3 to 4 minutes before serving, then garnish the dish with the chives or scallions.

KADOO GOSHT
Lamb with Chunks of Squash
SERVES 4

INGREDIENTS

¾ lb leg of lamb, boned

¾ lb squash

½–¾ tsp chili powder

¼ tsp turmeric

½ tsp Garam Masala (see page 18)

½ tsp ground coriander

1 tsp salt (optional)

2 tbsp oil

½ cup chopped onions

1 tbsp Ginger & Garlic Paste (see page 17)

½ cup chopped tomatoes

1 green chili, chopped

¼ cup chopped cilantro leaves

FOOD VALUE

	TOTAL	PER PORTION (¼)
TOTAL FAT	53.9 g	13.5 g
SATURATED FAT	17.4 g	4.4 g
CHOLESTEROL	277 mg	69 mg
ENERGY (calories)	842	210

This is light, summer curry. You might think a *summer* curry is odd, but the cool, clear-tasting squash does remind me of hot, summer days, and is delicious served on a mound of piping hot basmati rice.

You can use either braising steak or leg of lamb for this dish. Cook a little longer if you are using tougher cuts.

METHOD

1 Wash and cut the meat into 1-inch cubes.

2 Peel the squash, just taking off the skin and the minimum of flesh, and cut it into approximately 1-inch cubes.

3 Put the meat into a heavy-bottomed saucepan, add 1¼ cups of water and the chili powder, turmeric, Garam Masala, cilantro, if using, and salt along with the chopped onions and Ginger and Garlic Paste. Bring to a boil, reduce heat, cover, and simmer for 35 to 40 minutes.

4 Lift off the lid, turn up the heat, and stir continuously until the moisture has evaporated and the curry thickened a bit. Then add the oil and fry the spices well. Lower the heat and cook this mixture for 2 to 3 minutes, adding a small quantity of water whenever needed until the spices darken and glaze slightly.

5 Stir in the squash chunks and tomato. Add 1¼ cups of water, cover the pan, and cook for 10 to 12 minutes over a low heat. Add the green chili and half the cilantro leaves. Stir and cook for 2 to 3 minutes. Remove the pan from the heat, add the remaining cilantro leaves and let the dish stand for 3 to 4 minutes before serving.

GAJER GOSHT
Beef with Carrots and Peppers
SERVES 4

INGREDIENTS

¾ lb beef braising steak

½ lb carrots

¾ tsp chili powder

¼ tsp turmeric

½ tsp Garam Masala (see page 18)

1 tsp salt

⅓ cup chopped tomatoes

2 tbsp oil

1 tbsp lowfat plain yogurt

2 oz green bell pepper, sliced

1 green chili, chopped

½ tsp sugar

1 tbsp Ginger & Garlic Paste (see page 17)

2 cloves garlic, chopped or crushed

1 tbsp chopped mint leaves, to garnish

FOOD VALUE

	TOTAL	PER PORTION (¼)
TOTAL FAT	50 g	12.5 g
SATURATED FAT	14.5 g	3.6 g
CHOLESTEROL	158 mg	40 mg
ENERGY (calories)	791	198

This seemingly ordinary dish has a quite unusual, surprisingly delicious taste. The tomatoes and plain yogurt make this wonderfully tangy and it is a very convenient dish to make all year round.

METHOD

1 Cut the beef into 1-inch cubes.

2 Scrape, wash, and cut the carrots into tiny quarters by slicing the carrot lengthwise into 4 strips and then slicing across while holding the strips together.

3 Put the meat into a heavy-bottomed saucepan, add 1¼ cups of water, onions, Ginger and Garlic Paste, the chili powder, turmeric, Garam Masala, and salt. Bring it to a boil, then reduce the heat, cover and simmer for 35 to 40 minutes.

4 Now add the carrots, tomatoes, and yogurt, stirring them in well. Cover and cook for 8 to 10 minutes over a low heat. Then add the pepper, green chili, sugar, and chopped garlic. Stir to mix them in well. Cook for another 4 to 5 minutes. Remove the pan from the heat and serve, garnished with the mint leaves.

DAAL GOSHT
Lamb with Lentils
SERVES 4

INGREDIENTS

10 oz shoulder of lamb

½ cup red lentils

½ cup chopped onion

1 tbsp Ginger and Garlic Paste
(see page 17)

1 tsp chili powder

¼ tsp turmeric

½ tsp Garam Masala (see page 18)

1 tsp salt

1–2 green chilies, chopped

½ tsp cumin seeds, crushed

2 tbsp chopped cilantro leaves

FOOD VALUE

	TOTAL	PER PORTION (¼)
TOTAL FAT	25.7 g	6.4 g
SATURATED FAT	11.8 g	3 g
CHOLESTEROL	217 mg	54 mg
ENERGY (calories)	790	198

A family favorite all year round, you can use channa, maash, moong, masoor, or whatever type of lentil you happen to have. They each have a distinctive taste and flavor of their own so whenever you use a different one, you are creating a new dish with a special taste of its own. Here I am using masoor daal, or red lentil. It is easily available everywhere.

TO SERVE
The remarkable thing about this recipe is that no oil is used, which makes it especially low in fat.

METHOD
1 Wash and cut the meat into 1-inch cubes.

2 Wash and drain the lentils then put them into a small bowl and keep them to one side.

3 Put the meat in a heavy-bottomed saucepan, together with the onion, Ginger and Garlic Paste, chili powder, turmeric, and salt. Pour in 1 cup water, and bring it to a boil, then reduce the heat and cook, covered, for 20 to 25 minutes.

4 Now increase the heat and stir continuously until most of the moisture has evaporated.

5 Add the lentils, together with 2 cups of water and leave them to cook over a low heat for 30 to 35 minutes. Mix well with a wooden spoon during this time until they are thoroughly dissolved into the mixture and begin to look quite "mushy."

6 Add the Garam Masala, green chilies, and the cumin seeds, then simmer gently for another 3 to 4 minutes.

7 Add most of the cilantro leaves and stir to mix them in. Garnish with the reserved few leaves.

BHINDI GOSHT
Lamb with Okra and Onions
SERVES 4

INGREDIENTS

¾ lb lean shoulder of lamb

½ lb okra (prepared weight)

1 tsp chili powder

¼ tsp turmeric

½ tsp Garam Masala (see page 18)

1 tsp salt

1 tbsp Ginger and Garlic Paste
(see page 17)

1 cup sliced or chopped onion

2 tbsp oil

½ cup chopped tomatoes

½ tsp cumin seeds, crushed

a pinch of freshly ground black pepper

2 tsp lemon juice

FOOD VALUE

	TOTAL	PER PORTION (¼)
TOTAL FAT	55.8 g	13.9 g
SATURATED FAT	18.1 g	4.5 g
CHOLESTEROL	277 mg	69 mg
ENERGY (calories)	906	227

METHOD

1 Wash and cut the meat into 1-inch cubes.

2 Wash the okra and dry it well. (It is important to remove as much water as possible.) Trim the ends off and cut them into 2 or 3 pieces.

3 Put the meat into a medium-sized heavy-bottomed saucepan, add 1¼ cups of water and the chili powder, turmeric, Garam Masala, salt, and Ginger and Garlic Paste. Add, too, a third of the onion, reserving the rest for a later stage. Bring the mixture to a boil, then reduce the heat, cover and simmer for 25 to 30 minutes.

4 Be extra attentive during this stage as it is the most critical point in the cooking process. Remove the lid, then add the oil and stir continuously over a high heat until the liquid thickens to a paste, darkens a bit, and tiny wells of oil begin to appear, which will take 2 to 3 minutes. Keep adding a little water from time to time so the mixture cooks without sticking.

5 Stir in the okra, chopped green chili, tomatoes, and remaining onion. Cover and cook for 20 to 25 minutes over a low heat. You will find that the okra will release a sort of gummy substance, but it will soon be absorbed. Stir the mixture once lightly during this time. Lastly, sprinkle the cumin seeds, a grinding of black pepper, and the lemon juice over the top, then let it stand for a few minutes before serving.

A view from Agra's fort – Shah Jehan's palace and later his prison. The solace of his captivity was a distant view of the Taj.

BANGON GOSHT
Lamb with Eggplants
SERVES 4

INGREDIENTS

¾ lb leg of lamb

¾ lb eggplants

1 tsp chili powder

¼ tsp turmeric

½ tsp Garam Masala (see page 18)

1 tsp salt

⅔ cup chopped onion

2 tbsp oil

1 tbsp Ginger and Garlic Paste
(see page 17)

1–2 green chilies

⅓ cup chopped tomatoes

1 tbsp lowfat plain yogurt

1 tbsp Tamarind Pulp (see page 16),
(optional) or 2 tsp lemon juice

4–5 curry leaves (optional)

½ tsp sugar

½ tsp cumin seeds, crushed

2 cloves garlic, crushed

any green leaves (mint, cilantro, chives
or scallions), to garnish

FOOD VALUE

	TOTAL	PER PORTION (¼)
TOTAL FAT	55 g	13.8 g
SATURATED FAT	18 g	4.5 g
CHOLESTEROL	277 mg	69 mg
ENERGY (calories)	903	226

Traditionally, any remaining onions are fried before being added to the dish in the last stage of cooking, but we shall, of course, not do such a wicked thing!

METHOD

1 Wash and cut the lamb into 1-inch pieces.

2 Wash, dry, and slice the eggplants into quarters lengthwise, then, holding the strips together, cut them across into 1-inch chunks. Put the eggplant into a colander, sprinkle it generously with salt and leave it to stand for 40 to 50 minutes, until the bitter juices have run out. Rinse it under cold water, drain, and put to one side.

3 Put the meat into a medium-sized heavy-bottomed saucepan, add 1¼ cups of water, the chili powder, turmeric, Ginger and Garlic Paste, Garam Masala, salt and half the onions, reserving the rest for later. Bring the mixture to a boil, then reduce the heat, cover, and simmer for 25 to 30 minutes.

4 Be careful at this stage as it is crucial to the success of the dish. Remove the lid, add the oil, and stir continuously over a high heat until the liquid thickens to a paste, darkens a little, and tiny wells of oil appear, which takes 2 to 3 minutes. Add a little water from time to time to ensure that the mixture cooks without sticking.

5 Now add the eggplant, tomato, remaining onions, and yogurt. Mix them in well and let the mixture cook gently for a further 25 to 30 minutes, stirring occasionally during this time.

6 Add the Tamarind Pulp or lemon juice and curry leaves, if using. Also stir in the sugar, cumin seeds, and crushed garlic, then simmer for another 10 to 12 minutes. Garnish the dish with your chosen green leaves.

KEEMA MUTTER
Ground Meat with Peas and Peppers
SERVES 4

INGREDIENTS

¾ lb ground beef or lamb

⅔ cup sliced or chopped onion

½ cup chopped tomatoes

1 tbsp Ginger and Garlic Paste
(see page 17)

½–1 tsp chili powder

¼ tsp turmeric

½ tsp cumin seeds

½ tsp Garam Masala (see page 18)

1 tsp salt

1 cup fresh or frozen peas

1 green chili

2 tbsp chopped cilantro leaves or scallions

FOOD VALUE

	TOTAL	PER PORTION (¼)
TOTAL FAT	18.5 g	4.6 g
SATURATED FAT	7.2 g	1.8 g
CHOLESTEROL	207 mg	52 mg
ENERGY (calories)	587	147

Keema Mutter is a quick, easy, and versatile everyday dish. It is always handy to have in the refrigerator, too, for lovely snack meals or to fill sandwiches. You will notice that no oil has been used in this dish!

METHOD

1 Put the ground meat into a heavy-bottomed saucepan together with the onion, tomato, Ginger and Garlic Paste, chili powder, turmeric, cumin seeds, Garam Masala, and salt. Mix them well, cover the pan, and cook for 25 to 30 minutes over a low heat, stirring it occasionally during this time to make sure it does not catch.

2 Remove the lid and stir over a high heat to evaporate the excess liquid. Then add the peas and green chili. Cover and cook for a further 5 to 7 minutes.

3 Add half the cilantro leaves or scallions and cook for 2 to 3 more minutes. Remove the pan from the heat and garnish with the remaining cilantro or scallions.

KEEMA GOBHI
Ground Meat with Cauliflower

SERVES 4

INGREDIENTS

1 tbsp oil
3–4 whole dried chilies or 1 tsp chili powder
½ tsp cumin seeds
10 oz lean ground lamb or beef
½ cup chopped onion
¼ tsp turmeric
½ tsp Garam Masala (see page 18)
1 tsp salt
¾ lb cauliflower flowerets
⅓ cup chopped tomatoes
1 tbsp grated root ginger
3–4 fat cloves garlic, crushed or chopped
2–3 tbsp cilantro leaves (optional)

FOOD VALUE

	TOTAL	PER PORTION (¼)
TOTAL FAT	27.3 g	6.8 g
SATURATED FAT	7.3 g	1.8 g
CHOLESTEROL	162 mg	40.5 mg
ENERGY (calories)	596	149

METHOD

1 Heat the oil in a medium-sized heavy-bottomed saucepan. Add the dried chilies (do not put the chili powder in at this stage if you are using it instead) and cumin seeds. Fry these for 30 seconds over a medium heat, then add the ground meat and onions, stirring continuously.

2 Add the chili powder now, if using, the turmeric, Garam Masala, and salt and mix thoroughly. Cover, lower the heat, and simmer for 20 to 25 minutes.

3 Add the cauliflower, tomatoes, ginger, garlic, and the green chilies. Cook without a lid over a medium heat for 10 to 12 minutes. Once the moisture has evaporated, stir in the cilantro leaves, reserving some for garnishing.

DO PIAZA
Lamb with Twice the Amount of Onions

SERVES 4

INGREDIENTS

¾ lb shoulder of lamb
3–4 whole dried chilies
½-inch piece cinnamon stick
3–4 whole cloves
2 black cardamom pods, bruised (optional)
½ tsp peppercorns (optional)
1 tsp cumin seeds
2⅓ cups sliced onions
½ cup chopped tomatoes
1 tsp salt
2 tbsp oil
1 tbsp Ginger and Garlic Paste (see page 17)
2 green chilies, chopped

FOOD VALUE

	TOTAL	PER PORTION (¼)
TOTAL FAT	53.9 g	13.5 g
SATURATED FAT	17.4 g	4.4 g
CHOLESTEROL	277 mg	69 mg
ENERGY (calories)	926	232

This northern India dish has a unique taste and flavor all its own. The only thing is chopping up all those onions, but a well-made Do Piaza is an experience worth every tear!

METHOD

1 Wash and cut the lamb into 1-inch chunks.

2 Put the meat into a heavy-bottomed saucepan that has been greased with 1 tablespoon oil. Sprinkle all the whole spices over it, then the onions and tomatoes. Sprinkle the salt over, cover, and leave it to simmer gently for 30 minutes.

3 Give it a good stir, then add the remaining oil, Ginger and Garlic Paste, and green chilies. Cook uncovered, for another 15 minutes or until the moisture almost disappears.

4 Increase the heat and stir continuously so the onions become pulpy and the mixture takes on a slightly glazed look. Pick out the whole spices before serving, if preferred.

Ground Meat with Cauliflower.

KOFTA CURRY
Meatballs in Thick Gravy
SERVES 4

INGREDIENTS

KOFTAS

1 tbsp chick-pea flour, roasted, or cornstarch
½ cup chopped onions
2 tsp grated ginger root
3 fat garlic cloves
½ tsp chili powder
¼ tsp Garam Masala (see page 18)
½ tsp salt
3 tbsp chopped cilantro
1 green chili, finely chopped
¾ lb lean ground lamb or beef

SAUCE

2 tbsp oil
½ cup finely chopped onion
¼ tsp cumin seeds
2–3 green cardamoms
2 tsp Ginger and Garlic Paste (see page 17)
½ tsp chili powder
¼ tsp turmeric
¼ tsp Garam Masala (see page 18)
¾ tsp salt
⅓ cup chopped tomatoes
1 green chili, chopped
½ tbsp lowfat plain yogurt
2 tbsp chopped cilantro leaves

FOOD VALUE

	TOTAL	PER PORTION (¼)
TOTAL FAT	53.8 g	13.5 g
SATURATED FAT	17.5 g	4.4 g
CHOLESTEROL	277 mg	69 mg
ENERGY (calories)	952	238

Eastern herbs and spices work their magic best of all when the meat or poultry you want to use in a dish is marinated in them. In this recipe, the humble meatball is turned into something really special.

In the original recipe, roasted chick-pea flour and ground poppy seeds are used to bind and improve the texture of the meat, but, in my experience, using cornstarch instead of poppy seeds is simple and almost as effective.

METHOD

1 First make the koftas. If using chick-pea flour, dry roast it in a heavy-bottomed skillet, using a wooden spoon to move the flour around continuously until it changes to a slightly darker shade (2 to 3 minutes). Let it cool.

2 Grind the onion, ginger, garlic, cilantro leaves, and green chili in a blender.

3 Put the ground beef into a bowl and add all the above ingredients including the chili powder, Garam Masala, salt, and chick-pea flour or the cornstarch. Knead to mix them together thoroughly. Set the mixture to one side for 10 to 15 minutes for the spices to mingle.

4 Divide the mixture into 16 equal portions and, moistening the palm of your hand, roll each portion into a smooth round ball. Cook the koftas under a hot broiler for 10 minutes, turning them once, to drain off all the excess oil.

5 Now, make the sauce. Heat the oil in a medium-sized, heavy-bottomed saucepan. Add the onion and fry gently. Add the cumin seeds and cardamom pods. When the onion is deep, golden brown, add the Ginger and Garlic Paste, remaining spices, and salt. Cook this masala paste well, adding a little water when necessary, until the spices darken a little and tiny wells of oil appear on the surface of the mixture.

6 Add the tomatoes and yogurt and stir continuously.

7 Reduce the heat a little and drop the broiled koftas into the pan. Stir-fry some more, add 2 cups of water, then cover and cook for 20 to 25 minutes over a low heat.

8 Now add the green chili and cilantro leaves. The consistency of the sauce can be adjusted at this point cooking for a little longer to thicken it or by adding a little boiling water if you prefer a thinner sauce.

Kofta Curry.

VARIATION
KOFTA SAAG
Meatballs with Broccoli or Spinach
SERVES 4

Broccoli is my favorite vegetable and is really good for you, too. If you do not share my passion, you can easily substitute fresh spinach.

For this variation, use 10 ounces of ground meat instead and 1 pound of fresh broccoli (prepared weight), the rest of the ingredients remaining the same as left except that the cilantro is optional. Follow the method through step 7 but reserve the green chili and cilantro leaves, then continue as follows:

Reduce the heat and drop the broiled koftas into the pan. Add just 2–3 tablespoons of water and let the koftas soak up the spices by gently cooking them for 3 to 4 minutes. Add the broccoli and the green chili, cover, and simmer for 15 to 20 minutes, stirring occasionally during this time until the moisture disappears. Stir in the cilantro leaves just before serving. Adjust the consistency to your taste as above.

FOOD VALUE		
	TOTAL	**PER PORTION (¼)**
TOTAL FAT	39.8 g	10 g
SATURATED FAT	9 g	2.2 g
CHOLESTEROL	162 mg	40.5 mg
ENERGY (calories)	872	218

GOBHI GOSHT
Lamb with Cauliflower
SERVES 4

INGREDIENTS

1 lb cauliflower
¾ lb leg of lamb
2 tbsp oil
½ cup chopped onion
½ tsp cumin seeds
2 tsp Ginger and Garlic Paste (see page 17)
½ tsp chili powder
¼ tsp turmeric
1 tsp salt
⅓ cup chopped tomatoes
1 tsp grated ginger root
½ tsp Garam Masala (see page 18)
3 tbsp chopped cilantro
1 green chili, chopped

FOOD VALUE

	TOTAL	PER PORTION (¼)
TOTAL FAT	57.3 g	14.3 g
SATURATED FAT	18.3 g	4.6 g
CHOLESTEROL	277 mg	69 mg
ENERGY (calories)	958	239

A very popular everyday dish. Use only the freshest and crispiest cauliflower for the best results.

METHOD

1 Wash the cauliflower and drain it well. Discard the outer leaves and cut the cauliflower into small flowerets, including all the tender and crispy part of the vegetable, even the young leaves. Cut them into bite-sized pieces.

2 Wash and cut the lamb into 1-inch cubes.

3 Heat the oil in a medium-sized heavy-bottomed saucepan. Add the onion and fry it until it is translucent.

4 Add the ground coriander and cumin seeds. Stir-fry them for 30 seconds, then add the Ginger and Garlic Paste, chili powder, turmeric, and salt. Add 2 tablespoons of water and stir continuously. Repeat so the masala paste turns a shade darker.

5 Then, add the lamb and stir-fry this for 2 to 3 more minutes. Pour in 1 cup of water and let it come to the boil, then reduce the heat, cover and simmer for 20 to 25 minutes.

6 Increase the heat and stir continuously until all the excess moisture has evaporated and the mixture has a slightly glossy look.

7 Add the cauliflower, tomatoes, and ginger. Stir to blend everything together, cover and cook for 7 to 8 minutes.

8 Remove the lid, add the Garam Masala, half the cilantro leaves, and the green chili. Cook, uncovered, to let the liquid escape, turning the vegetables gently, for another 5 to 7 minutes or until the mixture is really quite dry. Use the remaining cilantro leaves to garnish.

Mild, Creamy Chicken Curry

Stir-fried Chicken with Tomatoes

Marinated Broiled Chicken

Chicken with Chick-peas

Chicken Dishes

Chicken with Spinach or Broccoli

MURGH KORMA
Mild, Creamy Chicken Curry
SERVES 4

INGREDIENTS

1 lb chicken breasts
1 tsp chili powder
1 tsp ground coriander
½ tsp Garam Masala (see page 18)
1 tsp salt
1 tbsp Ginger and Garlic Paste (see page 17)
2 tbsp oil
⅔ cup chopped onion
3–4 green cardamom pods, slit or bruised
½ tsp cumin seeds
2 tbsp lowfat plain yogurt
fresh mint ot chopped chives, to garnish

FOOD VALUE

	TOTAL	PER PORTION (¼)
TOTAL FAT	37.4 g	9.4 g
SATURATED FAT	7.6 g	1.9 g
CHOLESTEROL	198 mg	50 mg
ENERGY (calories)	812	203

Kormas are mostly rich and exotic. This recipe is for an ordinary, everyday korma, which is delicious even without all the usual trimmings of almonds, cream, and lashings of fried onions that normally go with it.

METHOD

1 Wipe, bone, and cut the chicken into 1-inch cubes.

2 Put the chili powder, ground coriander, Garam Masala, and salt, plus the Ginger and Garlic Paste into a little bowl. Add 4 tablespoons of hot water, mix and then put the mixture to one side.

3 Heat the oil in a medium-sized heavy-bottomed saucepan, add the onion, cardamom pods, and cumin seeds and fry them gently until the onion turns a deep golden brown.

4 Add the reserved spice mixture, stir it in well and keep cooking over a low heat, sprinkling tiny amounts of water in, if need be, until the paste darkens slightly, 2 to 3 minutes.

5 Add the chicken, coating it well in the spicy paste. Stir in the yogurt. Cover the pan and simmer for 10 minutes. The chicken will release its own moisture during this time so see how thick or runny the sauce is at the end of it and adjust it by adding water until it is how you like it. Then let it simmer over a low heat for 25 to 30 minutes. Garnish the finished dish with the mint or chives.

No matter what's been in them, all pots and pans are kept gleaming and clean.

KARAHI MURGH
Stir-fried Chicken with Tomatoes
SERVES 4

INGREDIENTS

1 lb chicken breasts	
1 cup chopped tomatoes	
½ tsp chili powder	
2 scallions, chopped	
2 green chilies, chopped	
1 tsp salt	
2 tbsp oil	
1 tsp cumin seeds	
2 tsp grated ginger root	
3–4 cloves garlic, crushed	
3 tbsp chopped cilantro leaves	

FOOD VALUE

	TOTAL	PER PORTION (¼)
TOTAL FAT	37.3 g	9.3 g
SATURATED FAT	7.3 g	1.8 g
CHOLESTEROL	194 mg	48 mg
ENERGY (calories)	767	192

A quick-and-easy dish to make, this originates from the northwest frontier of Pakistan. It is usually cooked in a wok-like utensil called a karahi, hence the name of the recipe.

METHOD

1 Wipe, bone, and cut the chicken into 1-inch pieces.

2 Put the chicken into a medium-sized heavy-bottomed saucepan. Cover the pan and leave it to cook in its own moisture over a low heat for about 10 minutes, stirring occasionally.

3 Add the tomatoes, chili powder, scallions, green chilies, and salt. Cook it, uncovered, over a medium heat for another 15 to 20 minutes or until the moisture has almost evaporated.

4 Heat the oil in a small skillet and cook the cumin seeds. As they begin to turn pink, add the ginger and garlic and fry these for about 1 minute. Add this sizzling mixture to the chicken, together with nearly all the cilantro leaves and mix them together well. Simmer for 5 to 7 minutes. Garnish the dish with the remaining cilantro leaves just before serving.

MURGH TIKKA
Marinated Broiled Chicken
SERVES 2

INGREDIENTS

2 × 6-oz chicken breast halves

1/3 cup chopped onion

2 tsp Ginger and Garlic Paste
(see page 17)

1 green chili

1 tbsp lowfat natural yogurt

1/4–1/2 tsp chili powder

1/4 tsp Garam Masala (see page 18)

pinch of ground mace

2 tsp lemon juice

2 tbsp chopped cilantro leaves

1/2 tsp salt

FOOD VALUE

	TOTAL	PER PORTION (1/2)
TOTAL FAT	8.5 g	4.2 g
SATURATED FAT	2.8 g	1.4 g
CHOLESTEROL	110 mg	55 mg
ENERGY (calories)	336	168

Probably the most popular and best-known dish in the Indian repertoire. As noted before, the skin is removed in most Indian dishes, but in this case no oil is used either, which makes it ideal for our purpose here. It is quite low in calories, too, so I thoroughly recommend that you enjoy it as often as possible.

METHOD

1 Wash, pat dry, and skin the chicken breasts. Score them diagonally across in 3 to 4 places.

2 Combine the remaining ingredients in an electric blender until you have a smooth paste.

3 Spread the spice paste over the chicken pieces, rubbing it well into them. Refrigerate the chicken, preferably overnight, but, if not, for at least 2 to 3 hours before cooking.

4 Just before you are ready to serve, cook them under a hot broiler for 4 to 5 minutes, then reduce the heat and continue cooking for another 15 to 20 minutes, turning them over halfway through.

MURGH CHANNA
Chicken with Chick-peas
SERVES 4

INGREDIENTS

1 lb chicken breasts

½ cup chopped onion

4 oz tomato

1 tbsp Ginger and Garlic Paste
(see page 17)

1 tsp salt

½–1 tsp chili powder

¼ tsp turmeric

½ tsp Garam Masala (see page 18)

1 tbsp oil

1⅓ cups canned chick-peas, drained

1–2 green chilies

½ tsp cumin seeds, crushed

1 tsp juliennes of fresh ginger

3 tbsp chopped cilantro leaves

2 tsp lemon juice

FOOD VALUE

	TOTAL	PER PORTION (¼)
TOTAL FAT	32.4 g	8.1 g
SATURATED FAT	6.6 g	1.7 g
CHOLESTEROL	194 mg	48 mg
ENERGY (calories)	924	231

This Punjabi invention was incredibly fashionable a few years ago, but, unlike a lot of fashions, this dish has remained popular, no doubt because of its wonderful taste and texture.

METHOD

1 Wash and skin the chicken, then cut it into 1-inch cubes

2 Put the chicken into a saucepan, with the onion, half the tomato, the Ginger and Garlic Paste, and salt. Cook over a low heat for 10 minutes or until the chicken releases its moisture, stirring occasionally.

3 Add the chili powder, turmeric, and Garam Masala and cook for a further 10 to 15 minutes.

4 Add the oil and cook the mixture uncovered until the moisture has almost all evaporated and has a slightly glazed look to it.

5 Add the chick-peas and green chilies. Mix them in well, then add

1 cup water. Bring it to a boil and simmer for 7 to 8 minutes.

6 Lastly, add the cumin seeds, juliennes of ginger, cilantro leaves, and the lemon juice. Simmer it for a couple more minutes, then garnish the dish with slices of tomatoes, cilantro leaves, or chopped scallions.

MURGH SAAG
Chicken with Spinach or Broccoli
SERVES 4

INGREDIENTS

1 lb chicken breasts
1 lb fresh spinach or broccoli
1 tbsp Ginger and Garlic Paste (see page 17)
2 oz fenugreek leaves (optional)
⅓ cup chopped onion
1 tsp chili powder
¼ tsp turmeric
½ tsp Garam Masala (see page 18)
½ tsp cumin seeds, crushed
1 tsp salt
2 tbsp oil
1½ tbsp lowfat plain yogurt
1 green chili

FOOD VALUE

	TOTAL	PER PORTION (¼)
TOTAL FAT	40.7 g	10.2 g
SATURATED FAT	8.3 g	2.1 g
CHOLESTEROL	197 mg	49 mg
ENERGY (calories)	893	223

A mainstay of home cooking, this dish pleases everyone in the family. A handful of fresh fenugreek leaves lends a unique, appetizing fragrance to the dish, so do use them if you can find any at an Asian grocery.

METHOD

1 Wash and skin the chicken and cut it into 1-inch cubes.

2 Wash the spinach in plenty of running water, carefully removing all the grit, then drain it well.

3 Roughly chop the leaves, discarding the stems.

4 Pour ½ cup of water into a medium-sized heavy-bottomed saucepan. Add the Ginger and Garlic Paste, the onion, chili powder, turmeric, Garam Masala, cumin seeds, and salt. Bring it to a boil, cover, and simmer for 5 minutes.

5 Drop the chicken pieces into the pan and simmer, uncovered, for 15 to 20 minutes, or until most of the moisture has evaporated.

6 Add the oil and cook over a higher heat, stirring continuously, until the food looks slightly glazed.

7 Add the yogurt, spinach or broccoli, the fenugreek, and the green chili. Blend everything well so that the spices coat the spinach evenly. Cover and cook over a low heat for about 10 minutes, or until the spinach releases its own moisture. Remove the lid and simmer uncovered. It is important to note that the Murgh Saag is not ready if it still looks a little watery. The finished dish must be almost dry with a hint of sheen to it.

Fish & Shrimp Dishes

Fish Curry

SERVES 4

2 tbsp oil
¼ tsp fenugreek seeds
½ tsp cumin seeds
⅓ cup finely chopped onions
½ tsp chili powder
¼ tsp turmeric
½ tsp Garam Masala (see page 18)
½ tsp ground coriander
½ tsp salt
2 tbsp lowfat plain yogurt
1 tbsp Ginger and Garlic Paste (see page 17)
1 lb haddock or cod, cut into 1 oz chunks
2 tbsp cilantro leaves
1–2 green chilies
Mint or chives, chopped, to garnish

FOOD VALUE

	TOTAL	PER PORTION (¼)
TOTAL FAT	26.1 g	6.5 g
SATURATED FAT	3.6 g	0.9 g
CHOLESTEROL	211 mg	53 mg
ENERGY (calories)	614	154

Fenugreek seeds give this curry a special flavor, but take care to use only the amount specified as they can make it bitter if used in any quantity.

METHOD

1 Heat the oil in a medium-sized heavy-bottomed saucepan. Drop in the fenugreek and cumin seeds and fry them for 30 seconds over a medium heat.

2 Add the onion and cook until it turns golden, stirring it from time to time to make sure it does not burn.

3 Blend the chili powder, turmeric, Garam Masala, ground coriander, and salt with the yogurt and then add this spice mixture to the onion. Stir and cook for a minute or so.

4 Add the Ginger and Garlic Paste and cook for a minute or so more. It is important to fry these spices well so that they begin to release their aroma as they darken slightly. Keep stirring, adding 1–2 tablespoons of water occasionally to keep the mixture from burning or sticking. Repeat 2 or 3 times.

5 Drop in the fish pieces, mixing them gently into the cooked masala. Add half the cilantro leaves and the green chili. Reduce the heat, shake the pan, cover, then let it simmer in its own moisture for 20 to 25 minutes, gently stirring or shaking the pan a couple of times during cooking.

6 Remove the pan from the heat and garnish with the remaining cilantro leaves and mint or chives.

KHUTI-MITHI MUCHHLI
Sweet-and-Sour Fish
SERVES 2

2 × 6 oz. fish fillets

(cod or haddock)

1–2 tbsp Tamarind Pulp (see page 16)

1 tbsp oil

¼ tsp mustard seeds

4–5 curry leaves (optional)

2 scallions, chopped

½ tsp grated ginger root

3 cloves garlic, crushed or chopped

¼ tsp Garam Masala (see page 18)

a pinch turmeric

½ tsp chili powder

small pinch ground coriander

½ tsp salt

1 tsp sugar

1 green chili, finely chopped

FOOD VALUE

	TOTAL	PER PORTION (½)
TOTAL FAT	13.7 g	6.8 g
SATURATED FAT	1.7 g	0.8 g
CHOLESTEROL	161 mg	80 mg
ENERGY (calories)	394	197

The sweet-and-sour taste is created by the liberal use of tamarind. If you cannot find tamarind, use vinegar or lemon juice instead.

METHOD

1 Cut the fish into 2-inch chunks and smother them with the tamarind pulp, to which has been added a pinch of salt. Set the fish to one side to marinate.

2 Heat the oil in a medium-sized heavy-bottomed saucepan. Add the mustard seeds and curry leaves, if using, and stir-fry them until they begin to crackle.

3 Add the scallions (reserving the pieces of green shoot). Soften the scallions, then add the ginger, garlic, Garam Masala, turmeric, chili powder, ground coriander, and salt. Cook this mixture well, adding 1 tablespoon of water from time to time until the masala paste turns slightly darker, 1 to 2 minutes.

4 Add the fish pieces, sugar, and green chili, stirring gently. Cover the pan and let the fish cook over a medium heat for 8 to 10 minutes, occasionally shaking the pan to make sure it does not stick (add a little more water if you prefer a runny sauce).

MUCHHLI AUR SUBZI
Fish with Vegetables
SERVES 4

1 lb fish, frozen or fresh haddock or cod
4 oz runner beans
2 tbsp oil
½ tsp mustard seeds
½ tsp cumin seeds
¼ tsp fenugreek seeds
1 tsp grated ginger root
4 oz cauliflower flowerets
3 oz tomatoes
½ tsp chili powder
¼ tsp turmeric
¼ tsp Garam Masala (see page 18)
½ tsp salt
3–4 cloves garlic, crushed
2 tsp lemon juice
1 green chili, chopped
2 tbsp cilantro leaves

FOOD VALUE

	TOTAL	PER PORTION (¼)
TOTAL FAT	26.8 g	6.7 g
SATURATED FAT	3.5 g	0.9 g
CHOLESTEROL	207 mg	52 mg
ENERGY (calories)	611	153

This is cooked Bengali style. Traditionally, mustard oil is used but, if you cannot find it, you can substitute any vegetable oil in its place. If you do use mustard oil, you must heat it to smoking point otherwise its pungent smell and taste will overpower the fish and can ruin the dish.

METHOD

1 Rinse and pat the fish dry. Cut it into 1-inch pieces.

2 Top and tail the beans and cut them into ½-inch pieces.

3 Heat the oil in a medium-sized heavy-bottomed saucepan and add the mustard, cumin, and fenugreek seeds. Stir-fry them until they begin to pop and splutter.

4 Add the ginger and fry it for 1 minute or so. Then add the beans, cauliflower, and tomatoes, mix them in and cook for a couple of minutes.

5 Add the chili powder, turmeric, Garam Masala, and salt, mix them well in, then cover the pan and cook over a low heat for 10 to 12 minutes.

6 Make a well in the center of the vegetables and gently drop in the fish pieces, then add the garlic, lemon juice, green chili, and half the cilantro leaves, then cover them with the vegetables. Simmer, covered, for 15 to 20 minutes, stirring gently halfway through.

7 Add the remaining cilantro leaves, shake the pan and let it stand for a couple of minutes before serving.

Goan Fish Curry

SERVES 4

INGREDIENTS

6–7 whole dried chilies
½ tsp coriander seeds
½ tsp cumin seeds
6–7 cloves garlic, crushed
½ tsp salt
1 tbsp shredded coconut
1 lb haddock or cod fillets
⅓ cup chopped onion
2 tbsp oil
1 tsp grated ginger root
⅓ cup chopped tomatoes
1–2 green chilies
1 tbsp Tamarind Pulp (see page 16) or vinegar

FOOD VALUE

	TOTAL	PER PORTION (¼)
TOTAL FAT	34.8 g	8.7 g
SATURATED FAT	11.3 g	2.8 g
CHOLESTEROL	207 mg	52 mg
ENERGY (calories)	661	165

Like most Goan curries, this dish is a bit hot. You can, of course, tame it according to your own taste simply by reducing the number of whole dried chilies you use.

METHOD

1 Grind the whole dried chilies, coriander and cumin seeds, garlic, and salt together to form a paste.
2 Soak the coconut in 4 tablespoons of warm water for 15 minutes.
3 Cut the fish into 1-inch pieces.
4 Sauté the onion in the oil over a medium heat until it turns golden brown. Add the spice paste and fry it well, adding a tiny amount of water frequently until it turns a slightly darker color, 1 to 2 minutes.

5 Add the grated ginger, chopped tomatoes, and green chilies. Mix them gently in, then drop in the fish pieces. Stir lightly to coat the fish pieces with the spices, then simmer for 5 minutes.
6 Add the soaked coconut and Tamarind Pulp or vinegar and let it simmer for 10 to 12 minutes, adding a little more liquid if you like a runny sauce or letting it cook uncovered for a couple more minutes if you prefer it thicker.

Fish Kabobs

SERVES 4

INGREDIENTS

14 oz fresh or frozen haddock or cod

2–3 tbsp chopped cilantro leaves, mint or chives

1 tbsp lemon juice

½-inch piece cinnamon stick

2–3 cloves

1 black cardamom pod, bruised (optional)

1 tsp grated ginger root

4 cloves garlic, crushed

¾ cup mashed potatoes

½ tsp chili powder

½ tsp salt

1 green chili, chopped

2 tsp oil

1 large egg, beaten

chopped scallion and wedges of fresh lemon, to garnish

FOOD VALUE

	TOTAL	PER PORTION (¼)
TOTAL FAT	15.2 g	1.9 g
SATURATED FAT	2.9 g	0.4 g
CHOLESTEROL	403 mg	50 mg
ENERGY (calories)	568	71

METHOD

1 Rinse the fish under running cold water.

2 Put the mint or chives into a small bowl, mix in the lemon juice and season, then put the mixture to one side.

3 In a small saucepan, put the cinnamon, cloves, and cardamom pod and ½ cup of slightly salted water, together with the ginger and garlic. Let it come to a boil gradually.

4 Put the fish into the spiced water and cook, uncovered, over a medium heat. Cook until the fish is tender and flakes easily and the water has completely evaporated. Leave it to cool, then discard the spices.

5 Flake the fish, removing any bones. Add the mashed potatoes, chili powder, salt, green chili, and cilantro leaves and mix them together.

6 Divide the mixture into 8 portions and roll each one into a neat ball with moistened hands. Make a dent in each ball, put a small quantity of the lemon mixture into it, cover the mixture then flatten into a burger shape. Keep them in the refrigerator until you are ready to serve them.

7 Grease a fairly large, preferably nonstick, skillet with half the oil. Dip each kabob into the beaten egg and put them into the hot pan. Fry them in 2 batches of 4, turning them only once. They should be completely heated through and look golden and crispy. Serve them piping hot, garnishing with the chopped cilantro or chives and a wedge of fresh lemon.

The beaches of Goa are amongst the most beautiful in the world. Its waters are plentiful in fish, and you will find the most delicious seafood dishes in this region.

MASALA MUCHHLI
Masala Fish
SERVES 2

INGREDIENTS

10 oz haddock or cod fish cutlets

1 tbsp oil

2 scallions

1 tsp Ginger and Garlic Paste
(see page 17)

1 tbsp lowfat plain yogurt

MARINADE

¼ tsp garlic powder

2 tsp lemon juice

freshly ground black pepper
and salt to taste

MASALA PASTE

8 fenugreek seeds

¼ tsp cumin seeds

1 tsp Ginger and Garlic Paste
(see page 17)

¼ tsp chili powder

a pinch turmeric

a pinch Garam Masala (see page 18)

1 tbsp lowfat plain yogurt

a pinch salt

1 tbsp cilantro leaves

lemon wedges, to garnish

FOOD VALUE

	TOTAL	PER PORTION (½)
TOTAL FAT	13.2 g	6.6 g
SATURATED FAT	1.8 g	0.9 g
CHOLESTEROL	106 mg	53 mg
ENERGY (calories)	307	153

METHOD

1 Put the fish in a shallow dish. Mix the marinade ingredients together and pour the mixture over the fish. Ensure the fish is well covered, then leave it to marinate in the refrigerator for at least 2 to 3 hours before cooking.

2 Heat the oil in a small saucepan. Add the cumin and fenugreek seeds and fry them for 1 minute. Then add all the other masala paste ingredients, except the cilantro and lemon wedges, and stir continuously. Add 1 tablespoon of water from time to time to stop it sticking and cook for at least 2 to 3 minutes. Lastly, add cilantro leaves and remove the pan from heat.

3 Just before serving, place the fish under a hot broiler for 8 to 10 minutes, turning once. Heat the masala paste and add 3 to 4 tablespoons of water. Let it come to a boil, stir in the scallions and switch off. Transfer the fish onto a serving plate, pour over the hot masala, and garnish with onion shoots or cilantro leaves and lemon wedges.

Broiled Masala Fish

SERVES 1

5 oz any white-fleshed fish, such as haddock or cod
1 tsp lemon juice
a pinch garlic powder
salt to taste
2 tsp lowfat plain yogurt
½ tsp Ginger and Garlic Paste (see page 17)
a pinch chili powder
a pinch Garam Masala (see page 18)
1 tbsp chopped cilantro leaves or mint
½ tsp oil
lemon wedges to garnish

FOOD VALUE

	TOTAL	SINGLE PORTION
TOTAL FAT		2.9 g
SATURATED FAT		0.5 g
CHOLESTEROL		70 mg
ENERGY (calories)		146

After being marinated, this fish is traditionally deep- or shallow-fried, but it is still delicious when just lightly brushed with oil and cooked under a hot broiler.

METHOD

1 Rinse and pat the fish dry.

2 Mix the lemon juice, garlic powder, and a pinch of salt together and rub this mixture over the fish.

Leave in the refrigerator for 15 to 20 minutes.

3 Combine the yogurt, Ginger and Garlic Paste, chili powder, Garam Masala, mint or cilantro leaves, reserving a little for garnishing, and a little salt. Add the oil to this masala paste and blend thoroughly.

4 Coat the fish, on both sides, with the masala paste and leave it to marinate a second time in the refrigerator for at least 1 hour.

5 Put the fish under a hot broiler and cook for 4 to 5 minutes on each side. Garnish with the lemon wedges and reserved mint or cilantro leaves.

Spicy Sardine Spread

SERVES 2

INGREDIENTS

4 oz sardines in tomato sauce

2 green chilies, thinly sliced

2–3 cloves garlic, finely chopped

2 scallions

1 tbsp mint or cilantro leaves

a pinch freshly ground black pepper

1 tsp vinegar or lemon juice

a pinch salt

⅓ cup chopped onion

¾ cup chopped cucumber

FOOD VALUE

	TOTAL	PORTION (½)
TOTAL FAT	12 g	6 g
SATURATED FAT	3.3 g	1.6 g
CHOLESTEROL	76 mg	38 mg
ENERGY (calories)	211	105

No cooking is required for this instantaneous, simple and "just out of the larder" spread. I invent things like this on an impulse, wanting to get the best out of simple ingredients with the minimum fuss.

METHOD

1 Flake the sardines into a bowl and add the green chilies, garlic, scallions, mint or cilantro leaves, and freshly ground pepper.

2 Pour the vinegar or lemon juice over the sardine mixture. Sprinkle the salt onto the onion and cucumber and add these to the sardine mixture, too. Mix thoroughly. This is delicious on toasted bread, or as a sandwich filling.

JHINGA ALOO

Shrimp with Potatoes

SERVES 4

INGREDIENTS

¾ lb fresh or frozen shrimp

1 tbsp lemon juice

¼ tsp garlic powder or fresh crushed garlic

½ lb potatoes

2 tbsp oil

¼ tsp fenugreek seeds

½ tsp cumin seeds

½ cup chopped tomatoes

½ tsp chili powder

¼ tsp turmeric

¼ tsp Garam Masala (see page 18)

1–2 green chilies, chopped

2 tsp Ginger & Garlic Paste (see page 17)

½ tsp salt

3 tbsp chopped cilantro leaves

FOOD VALUE

	TOTAL	PER PORTION
TOTAL FAT	29.2 g	7.3 g
SATURATED FAT	4.2 g	1.05 g
CHOLESTEROL	284 mg	71 mg
ENERGY (calories)	762	191

METHOD

1 Rinse and pat the shrimp dry.

2 Mix the lemon juice and garlic powder or fresh garlic together and coat the shrimp with the mixture. Leave them to marinate, refrigerated, for 20 minutes.

3 Chop the potatoes into ½-inch dice, preferably with skins.

4 Heat the oil in a medium-sized heavy-bottomed saucepan, then add the fenugreek and cumin seeds, letting them sizzle for 30 seconds.

5 Add the Ginger and Garlic Paste and cook for 30 seconds, then add the potato and tomato. Stir and cook them for 2 minutes.

6 Now add the marinated shrimp. Mix them in and, immediately, add the chili powder, turmeric, Garam Masala, green chilies, and salt. Mix thoroughly, then add ⅔ cup of hot water. Cover the pan and simmer for 8 to 10 minutes, or until the potato is just tender – do not let them become overdone.

7 Add half the cilantro leaves, stirring them into the curry and cook for a minute or 2.

8 Sprinkle the remaining cilantro leaves over the top to garnish and remove the pan from the heat.

BHOONA JHINGA
Dry Masala Shrimp
SERVES 4

INGREDIENTS

½ tsp cumin seeds
½ tsp coriander seeds
1 tsp aniseed
3–4 whole dried chilies
4–5 cloves garlic, chopped
1–2 green chilies, chopped
⅓ cup chopped onion
2 tbsp cilantro leaves
2 tbsp oil
¼ tsp fenugreek seeds
1 lb shrimp
3 oz tomatoes
1 tbsp lowfat plain yogurt
¼ tsp turmeric
cilantro or mint leaves, to garnish

FOOD VALUE

	TOTAL	PER PORTION (¼)
TOTAL FAT	30.8 g	7.7 g
SATURATED FAT	4.8 g	1.2 g
CHOLESTEROL	367 mg	92 mg
ENERGY (calories)	739	185

An absolutely delicious south-Indian shrimp dish.

METHOD

1 Dry roast the cumin and coriander seeds and aniseed in a small, heavy-bottomed skillet over a low heat for a couple of minutes, then leave them to cool. Grind them together with the whole dried chilies, garlic, green chilies, onion, and cilantro leaves.

2 Heat the oil in a heavy-bottomed saucepan and fry the fenugreek seeds for 30 seconds. Add the shrimp, tomato, and yogurt. Cook over a high heat for 1 minute to seal them.

3 Now add the ground spice mixture and the turmeric. Mix them in well and fry for another minute.

4 Add ½ cup of water and bring to a boil. Lower the heat and simmer for 5 to 7 minutes. Garnish with 1 tablespoon mint or cilantro leaves.

Goan Shrimp Curry

SERVES 4

INGREDIENTS

3–4 whole dried chilies
¼ tsp peppercorns
½ tsp cumin seeds
1 tsp coriander seeds
1 tbsp fresh or shredded coconut
4–5 cloves garlic, chopped
2 tbsp oil
3 oz onions
3 oz tomatoes
2 tsp grated ginger root
1–2 green chilies
2 tbsp Tamarind Pulp (see page 16) or 1 tbsp vinegar
1 lb shrimp
2 tbsp chopped cilantro leaves

FOOD VALUE

	TOTAL	PER PORTION (¼)
TOTAL FAT	39.8 g	10 g
SATURATED FAT	12.6 g	3.2 g
CHOLESTEROL	365 mg	91 mg
ENERGY (calories)	810	202

I was first introduced to this dish by my Goan friend at an office party, and it soon became one of our family favorites. It may well become one of your favorites, too! This is, of course, slightly modified to reduce the calories but I still find it tasty enough to want you to try it. The original recipe calls for huge amounts of fresh, grated coconut, but I find that just the single spoonful used here is satisfying enough.

METHOD

1 Grind together the whole dried chilies, peppercorns, and cumin and coriander seeds. Then add the coconut and garlic and grind some more.

2 Heat the oil in a medium-sized saucepan and fry the onions over low heat. As they begin to turn translucent, add the ginger and green chilies and cook for 30 seconds. Add the spice paste, with the salt, mix this masala in and fry it for about 1 minute, adding a little water.

3 Add the Tamarind Pulp or vinegar stirring continuously for 30 seconds.

4 Stir in the shrimp and tomatoes and coat them well in the sauce. Add ½ to ¾ cup of water and let the curry cook for 5 minutes over a medium heat.

5 Add most of the cilantro leaves and simmer for another 5 to 7 minutes. Garnish with the remaining cilantro leaves.

JHINGA SUBZI
Shrimp Curry with Vegetables
SERVES 4

INGREDIENTS

10 oz fresh or frozen shrimp
3 oz fresh or frozen green beans
2 tbsp oil
1/3 cup finely chopped onion
1 tsp grated ginger root
1/2 tsp chili powder
1/4 tsp turmeric
1/4 tsp Garam Masala (see page 18)
1 tsp salt
4 tbsp chopped tomato
1/2 cup chopped red bell peppers
3 oz button mushrooms
3–4 cloves garlic, chopped
1–2 green chilies, chopped
1/2 tsp sugar
1 tbsp lowfat plain yogurt
2 tbsp chopped cilantro leaves

FOOD VALUE

	TOTAL	PER PORTION (1/4)
TOTAL FAT	28.6 g	7.2 g
SATURATED FAT	4.2 g	1 g
CHOLESTEROL	225 mg	56 mg
ENERGY (calories)	595	149

You can choose your own combination of vegetables for this dish – just adjust the calories for the selected vegetables.

METHOD

1 If using fresh shrimp, rinse and pat them dry.

2 If using fresh green beans, wash and cut them into small bite-size pieces.

3 Heat the oil in a medium-sized heavy-bottomed saucepan and fry the onion and, as it turns translucent, add the ginger, chili powder, turmeric, Garam Masala, and salt. Mix well and cook for a few seconds.

4 Now add the tomato, red pepper, and mushrooms, stir and cook for 5 to 7 minutes over a medium heat.

5 Add the shrimp, garlic, green chilies, sugar, and yogurt. Mix well and cook over a medium heat for 7 to 8 minutes.

6 Add the cilantro leaves and simmer for another couple of minutes.

BHINDI JHINGA
Shrimp with Okra
SERVES 4

INGREDIENTS

3/4 lb okra (prepared weight)
2 tbsp oil
4 oz onions
2–3 whole dried chilies
1/2 tsp cumin seeds
4 cloves garlic, chopped
1/4 tsp turmeric
1/2 tsp chili powder
1/2 cup chopped tomatoes
1/2 lb shrimp
1–2 green chilies, slit
1 tsp salt
2 tbsp Tamarind Pulp (see page 16)
2 tbsp chopped cilantro leaves

FOOD VALUE

	TOTAL	PER PORTION (1/4)
TOTAL FAT	27.8 g	7 g
SATURATED FAT	4 g	1 g
CHOLESTEROL	450 mg	113 mg
ENERGY (calories)	523	131

METHOD

1 Rinse and pat the okra dry. Top and tail them and chop them into 1/2-inch wide slices.

2 Heat the oil and lightly fry the onion with the dried chilies and cumin seeds and then add the garlic, turmeric, chili powder, and ginger. Stir them together well and cook the mixture for a couple of minutes, stirring continuously.

3 Add the okra and tomato, coat them well with the spices, cover the pan and simmer gently for 5 to 7 minutes, stirring occasionally.

4 Stir in the shrimp, chopped or slit green chilies, and salt. Cook for another 5 minutes, then add the Tamarind Pulp or lemon juice and cilantro leaves. Shake the pan and simmer for 5 more minutes. Then, turn off the heat and let it stand for 2 to 3 minutes before serving.

Shrimp with Okra.

JHINGA SAAG
Shrimp with Broccoli or Spinach
SERVES 4

INGREDIENTS

1 lb broccoli or fresh spinach

2 tsp Ginger and Garlic Paste
(see page 17)

2 tbsp oil

1/3 cup finely chopped onion

1/4 tsp cumin seeds

2 cloves garlic, finely chopped

1/2 tsp chili powder

1/4 tsp turmeric

1/2 tsp Garam Masala (see page 18)

3/4 tsp salt

10 oz fresh or frozen shrimp

1 tbsp lowfat plain yogurt

4 tbsp chopped tomato

FOOD VALUE

	TOTAL	PER PORTION (1/4)
TOTAL FAT	31.7 g	7.9 g
SATURATED FAT	4.9 g	1.2 g
CHOLESTEROL	225 mg	56 mg
ENERGY (calories)	695	174

METHOD

1 If using fresh shrimp, rinse and pat them dry.

2 Rinse and chop the broccoli or spinach.

3 Put the broccoli or spinach into a medium-sized saucepan and add the Ginger and Garlic Paste, a pinch of salt, and 1/2 cup of water. Cook, uncovered, over a low heat until the broccoli or spinach is tender and almost all of the liquid has evaporated.

4 Heat the oil in another medium-sized heavy-bottomed saucepan. Fry the onion and cumin seeds until they change to a pale gold color.

5 Add the garlic and cook for 30 seconds, then add the chili powder, turmeric, Garam Masala, and salt. Cook this mixture for another minute or so, adding 1 tablespoon of water as necessary to avoid the mixture burning or sticking, and stir continuously.

6 Add the shrimp and then the yogurt. Stir-fry everything together for 30 seconds.

7 Add the tomato, mix it in and cook over a low heat for 2 to 3 minutes. Combine the cooked broccoli with the shrimp mixture and cook over a medium heat for another 8 to 10 minutes.

60

Greens with Garlic butter

Mixed Vegetable Bhaji

Green Beans with Potatoes

Seasonal Vegetables in Green Masala

Vegetable Dishes

Cabbage and Carrot Bhaji

Eggplant with Potatoes

Mushroom, Leek, and Pepper Bhaji

Quick Crunchy Bhaji

Broken Potatoes with Spices

Peas and Mushroom Bhaji

Cauliflower Steamed with Herbs and Spices

Chunks of Potatoes with Fresh Spinach

PHALLI ALOO
Green Beans with Potatoes
SERVES 4

INGREDIENTS

14 oz green beans

7 oz potatoes

2 tbsp oil

½ tsp cumin seeds

3–4 whole dried chilies or
½ tsp chili powder

⅓ cup chopped tomato

1–2 green chilies

¼ tsp turmeric

salt to taste

FOOD VALUE

	TOTAL	PER PORTION (¼)
TOTAL FAT	24.6 g	6.2 g
SATURATED FAT	3.1 g	0.8 g
CHOLESTEROL	0	0
ENERGY (calories)	457	114

METHOD

1 Top and tail the green beans and chop them into small pieces.

2 Scrub the potatoes and dice finely, preferably keeping the skin on.

3 Heat the oil, add the cumin seeds and break in the whole dried chilies. (If using the chili powder, do not add it yet.)

4 As soon as the dried chilies darken (this just takes a minute or so), add the beans, tomato, and green chilies. Cook for a couple of minutes, then add the potato. Add the chili powder now, if using, together with the turmeric and salt. Cover and simmer for 15 minutes.

Seasonal Vegetables in Green Masala
SERVES 4

INGREDIENTS

½ lb cauliflower

¼ lb green beans

¼ lb carrots

¼ lb red or green bell peppers

¼ lb tomatoes

2 green chilies

3 tbsp cilantro leaves

2 tbsp oil

3–4 whole dried chilies

1 tsp cumin seeds

¼ tsp turmeric

½–¾ tsp salt

2 tsp grated ginger root

4–5 fat cloves garlic, chopped

FOOD VALUE

	TOTAL	PER PORTION (¼)
TOTAL FAT	25.4 g	6.4 g
SATURATED FAT	3.4 g	0.8 g
CHOLESTEROL	0	0
ENERGY (calories)	364	91

I have chosen four vegetables, but you can substitute any you prefer or happen to have. If one of them happens to be potatoes, however, remember that they are higher in calories, but this dish is quite low in calories so, if you are not watching them too closely, this will be all right.

METHOD

1 Remove the outer leaves from the cauliflower and cut it into flowerets.

2 Top and tail and string the green beans, then chop them into bite-size pieces.

3 Scrape, wash, and dice the carrots.

4 Cut the peppers into tiny squares.

5 Chop the tomatoes, green chilies, and cilantro leaves.

6 Heat the oil in a medium-sized heavy-bottomed saucepan. Break and drop the whole dried chilies into the pan (do not put the chili powder in yet, if using) together with the cumin seeds and, within a minute of adding these, add all the vegetables, but not the green chilies or cilantro leaves. At the same time, add the turmeric, chili powder, if using, and salt. Cook for a minute or so while stirring the vegetables together.

7 Now add the ginger, garlic, green chilies, and cilantro leaves (which together are the green masala). Stir continuously until the ingredients are well mixed. Cover the pan and simmer over a medium heat for 15 minutes, until the vegetables are just slightly underdone.

Seasonal Vegetables in Green Masala.

Cabbage and Carrot Bhaji

SERVES 4

INGREDIENTS

2 tbsp oil
1 tbsp coriander seeds, crushed
½ tsp cumin seeds
2–3 whole dried chilies
4 cups shredded cabbage
1 cup diced carrots
⅓ cup chopped tomatoes
¼ tsp turmeric
1 green chili, chopped
½ tsp salt

FOOD VALUE

	TOTAL	PER PORTION (¼)
TOTAL FAT	24 g	6 g
SATURATED FAT	3 g	0.8 g
CHOLESTEROL	0	0
ENERGY (calories)	350	88

This is a sheer blessing for slimmers! It is very simple and quick to make and tastes really good. It is a money, time and calorie saver – what more can one ask for?

METHOD

1 Heat the oil in a medium-sized heavy-bottomed saucepan and stir in the coriander and cumin seeds and whole dried chilies. (If using chili powder instead, do not add it at this stage.) Fry these over a medium heat for 1 minute, or until the chilies and seeds darken slightly.

2 Add the cabbage, carrot, and tomatoes, then the turmeric, chili powder, if using, green chilies, and salt. Stir to mix everything together thoroughly.

3 Reduce the heat, cover, and simmer for 15 to 20 minutes. The vegetables should be on the very edge of tender with a little crunch to them, but if you like your vegetables softer, cook them for a little longer.

Vegetable vendors compete fiercely to sell their produce.

BANGON ALOO
Eggplant with Potatoes
SERVES 4

¾ lb eggplant	
½ lb potatoes	
2 tbsp oil	
⅓ cup sliced onion	
½ tsp cumin seeds	
½ tsp Roasted and Crushed Coriander Seeds (see page 18)	
3–4 curry leaves (optional)	
1 tsp grated ginger root	
4–5 cloves garlic, finely chopped	
½ tsp chili powder	
¼ tsp turmeric	
salt to taste	
1 tbsp lowfat plain yogurt	
½ tsp sugar	
1–2 green chilies, chopped	
⅓ cup chopped tomato	
1 tbsp lemon juice	
2 tbsp chopped cilantro leaves	

FOOD VALUE

	TOTAL	PER PORTION (¼)
TOTAL FAT	24.8 g	6.2 g
SATURATED FAT	3.3 g	0.8 g
CHOLESTEROL	2 mg	0.5 mg
ENERGY (calories)	496	124

METHOD

1 Wash the eggplant. Cut it into quarters lengthwise, then, holding the pieces together, cut them across into ½-inch chunks.

2 Scrub the potatoes thoroughly and do not peel them, then cut each one into quarters and each quarter twice or more so that you have at least 12 bite-size pieces from each potato.

3 Heat the oil in a medium-sized heavy-bottomed saucepan and fry the onion until it turns light brown.

4 Add the cumin and coriander seeds and the curry leaves, if using. Fry these for a minute or so, then add the ginger, half the garlic, the chili powder, turmeric, and salt. Cook this mixture over quite a high heat, adding 2 tablespoons of water as necessary so that the spice paste deepens in color and does not stick. This should not take longer than 2 minutes.

5 Add the eggplant, then the yogurt, sugar, and green chilies. Mix everything together and cook for 2 to 3 minutes. Add ⅔ cup of water, lower the heat and simmer for 15 minutes, with the lid firmly on.

6 Add the potato, peppers, and tomato. Ensuring that the lid is firmly on, simmer for another 10 minutes, checking it occasionally to make sure that it is not sticking or burning. If it seems a bit too dry or you would prefer a little more sauce, just add a little more water and let it simmer for a few more minutes.

7 Lastly, add the remaining garlic, the lemon juice, and cilantro leaves. Cook for 1 more minute, gently stir to mix it thoroughly, then turn off the heat.

Mushroom, Leek, and Pepper Bhaji

SERVES 4

INGREDIENTS

¾ lb mushrooms (prepared weight)

2 oz leek

2 tsp coriander seeds

½ tsp cumin seeds

3 tbsp oil

2 tsp lowfat plain yogurt

3–4 plump cloves garlic, finely chopped

⅓ cup sliced red bell pepper

⅓ cup sliced green bell pepper

½ tsp chili powder

¼ tsp turmeric

½ tsp salt

4 tbsp chopped tomato

1–2 green chili, very finely chopped

2 tbsp cilantro leaves

FOOD VALUE

	TOTAL	PER PORTION (¼)
TOTAL FAT	35.9 g	9 g
SATURATED FAT	4.6 g	1.2 g
CHOLESTEROL	1.3 mg	0.3 mg
ENERGY (calories)	403	101

METHOD

1 Wipe the mushrooms clean and pull out their stems. Cut the small mushrooms in half and the large ones into quarters.

2 Wash the leek thoroughly and cut into ¼-inch thick slices.

3 Crush the coriander seeds with a rolling pin and set them to one side.

4 Add the coriander and cumin seeds to the oil, which has been heated in a pan, and let them sizzle for 30 seconds over a medium heat.

5 Add the yogurt, garlic, and the prepared vegetables. Stir to mix everything together, then cook for 1 to 2 minutes.

6 Add the chili powder, turmeric, and salt, stirring continuously as you do so.

7 Add the tomato and green chili and cook, uncovered, over a medium heat for 8 to 10 minutes, stirring from time to time and evaporating as much moisture as possible.

8 Add half the cilantro leaves, stirring them into the mixture, then garnish the dish with the remaining leaves.

The Taj Mahal at dawn.

Quick, Crunchy Bhaji

SERVES 4

INGREDIENTS

¼ lb cauliflower

¼ lb green beans

¼ lb red and green bell peppers

3 tbsp oil

3–4 whole dried chilies,
broken roughly

1 tsp cumin seeds

¼ tsp turmeric

½ tsp salt

¼ lb carrots

heaped ⅓ cup chopped tomatoes

2 tsp grated ginger root

3–4 plump cloves garlic, chopped or
crushed

1 green chili, chopped

2–3 tbsp chopped cilantro leaves

FOOD VALUE

	TOTAL	PER PORTION (¼)
TOTAL FAT	35.3 g	8.8 g
SATURATED FAT	4.5 g	1.1 g
CHOLESTEROL	0	0
ENERGY (calories)	421	105

METHOD

1 Cut the cauliflower into small flowerets.

2 Trim the green beans and cut each one into 3–4 pieces.

3 Cut the red and green peppers into small squares.

4 Scrub and dice the carrots.

5 Heat the oil in a medium-sized heavy-bottomed pan, then add the whole dried chilies, breaking them into the pan, and the cumin seeds. As they begin to sizzle, add the turmeric and salt. Stir, then add all the vegetables, including the tomato. Mix and simmer for 2 minutes.

6 Add the ginger, garlic, and green chilies and stir to blend everything together thoroughly.

7 Then, lower the heat, cover the pan tightly and steam cook the vegetables for 12–15 minutes.

8 Finally, add the cilantro leaves, then serve.

ALOO KA BHURTA
Broken Potatoes with Spices
SERVES 4

INGREDIENTS

¾ lb potatoes
2 tbsp oil
½ cup chopped onions
½ tsp cumin seeds
2–3 whole dried chilies, broken
¼ tsp turmeric
⅓ cup chopped tomatoes
1 green chili, chopped
½ tsp salt
3 tbsp chopped cilantro leaves

FOOD VALUE

	TOTAL	PER PORTION (¼)
TOTAL FAT	23.2 g	5.8 g
SATURATED FAT	2.7 g	0.7 g
CHOLESTEROL	0	0
ENERGY (calories)	519	130

METHOD

1 Boil the potatoes in their skins and leave them to cool. Then, peel and break them into a lumpy mash. If preferred, peel potatoes first and then boil.

2 Heat the oil in a medium-sized heavy-bottomed saucepan and add the onion, cumin seeds, and whole dried chilies, breaking them into the pan. Fry until the onions turn a rich, golden brown.

3 Add the mashed potato. Sprinkle in, and mix well after each addition, the turmeric, tomato, green chili, and salt. Blend in ¾-1 cup of water and leave the mixture to cook over a low heat until it begins to bubble.

4 Add half the cilantro leaves, stir, and cook for another 30 seconds. Garnish the dish with the remaining cilantro leaves.

Exotic herbs and spices are a colorful and common sight in towns across India. The chief skill in their use lies in the subtle blending of fiery spices to enhance, rather than overwhelm, the flavor of the finished dish.

MUTTER MUSHROOM BHAJI
Peas and Mushroom Bhaji
SERVES 4

INGREDIENTS

14 oz button mushrooms
⅓ cup finely sliced onion
2 tbsp oil
¼ tsp cumin seeds, crushed
¼ tsp mustard seeds
heaped ⅓ cup chopped tomatoes
1 green chili, very finely chopped
1 cup frozen peas
½ tsp chili powder
¼ tsp turmeric
½ tsp salt
⅔ cup chopped red bell pepper
4 fat cloves garlic, crushed
2 tbsp cilantro leaves
chopped scallions or chives, to garnish

FOOD VALUE

	TOTAL	PER PORTION (¼)
TOTAL FAT	26.9 g	6.7 g
SATURATED FAT	3.6 g	0.9 g
CHOLESTEROL	0	0
ENERGY (calories)	425	106

METHOD

1 Wipe mushrooms clean, slice off the stems and cut the small mushrooms into halves and the large ones into quarters.

2 Fry the onions gently in the oil and, as they begin to turn a bit pulpy, add the cumin and mustard seeds. Fry for another couple of minutes.

3 Add the tomato and green chili, followed by the mushrooms and peas. Stir and cook them for a couple of minutes over a medium heat.

4 Add the chili powder, turmeric, and salt, mixing them in well, and cook, uncovered, for 5 to 7 minutes.

5 Finally, stir in the red pepper, garlic, and cilantro leaves and cook for another 5 minutes until the mixture is quite dry. Garnish with the chopped scallions or chives.

DUM GOBHI
Cauliflower Steamed with Herbs and Spices
SERVES 4

INGREDIENTS

1 lb cauliflower

½ tsp chili powder

¼ tsp turmeric

2 tsp grated ginger root

⅓ cup chopped tomatoes

1 green chili, chopped

½–¾ tsp salt

1 tbsp lowfat plain yogurt

2 tbsp oil

2–3 tbsp chopped cilantro leaves

½ tsp Garnishing Garam Masala
(see page 18)

FOOD VALUE

	TOTAL	PER PORTION (¼)
TOTAL FAT	26.7 g	6.7 g
SATURATED FAT	3.9 g	1 g
CHOLESTEROL	2 mg	0.5 mg
ENERGY (calories)	392	98

This is simple but superb and so low in calories. Make it frequently, serving it with other heavier dishes or on its own at the end of a "sinful" day.

METHOD

1 Wash, drain, and cut the cauliflower into small, even-sized flowerets (about 1 inch), including the stems.

2 Combine the chili powder and turmeric, ginger, tomato, green chili, and salt with the yogurt in a small bowl.

3 Grease the inside of a medium-sized saucepan liberally with the oil. Put the cauliflower into the saucepan, then pour the spice and yogurt mixture over it. Cover the pan tightly and cook over a low heat for 10 to 15 minutes (the cauliflower will steam-cook in the spicy mixture).

4 Stir in half the cilantro leaves, increase the heat to medium, and cook with the lid off, shaking the pan or stirring gently from time to time, for another 5 to 6 minutes, driving off the excess moisture.

5 Turn off the heat and sprinkle the Garnishing Garam Masala and the remaining cilantro leaves over the top. Give the pan one final shake, making sure that there is no moisture left. Cook it for a little longer, uncovered, if there is, as a watery Dum Gobhi will not taste right.

PALAK ALOO
Chunks of Potato Cooked with Fresh Spinach
SERVES 4

INGREDIENTS

14 oz fresh or frozen leaf spinach

½ lb potatoes

2 tbsp oil

¼ tsp fenugreek seeds

½ tsp cumin seeds

scant ⅓ cup chopped tomato

¼ tsp turmeric

½ tsp chili powder

salt to taste

FOOD VALUE

	TOTAL	PER PORTION (¼)
TOTAL FAT	25.9 g	6.5 g
SATURATED FAT	3.1 g	0.8 g
CHOLESTEROL	0	0
ENERGY (calories)	477	119

This is one of my favorite bhajis, especially if a bunch of fresh fenugreek leaves is added to it. These leaves are called methi and can be obtained from most Asian grocers all year round, but as these shops are not located everywhere, I have left them out of the recipe. If you do find some, just remove the leaves from the hard, stringy stems and substitute these for 2 ounces of the spinach. The leaves are highly aromatic and even this small quantity is enough to infuse the whole dish with its distinct, appetizing flavor.

Measure the fenugreek seeds carefully as any more will give the dish a bitter taste.

METHOD

1 If you are using fresh spinach, weigh it after you have removed the stems and chopped it. Wash it thoroughly to remove all the hidden dirt and leave it to drain in a colander. If you are using frozen spinach, defrost it and let it drain well in a colander.

2 Scrub the potatoes well and do not peel them. Cut the potatoes into quarters, then cut each quarter into 2 or more pieces, making 8 to 12 pieces from each potato.

3 Heat the oil in a medium-sized heavy-bottomed saucepan and fry the fenugreek and cumin seeds. As the seeds begin to sizzle, add the tomato, turmeric, chili powder, and salt. Mix and cook the mixture for 30 seconds.

4 Add the spinach and potato and mix well so that the vegetables become well coated in the spices.

5 Cover the pan and simmer for 15 to 20 minutes. If there is still a little moisture left after this time, remove the lid and dry it out a little by cooking rapidly over a medium to high heat for another few minutes, taking great care not to let it burn.

Lentils & Beans

Buttered Red Lentils

SERVES 4

scant 1 cup red lentils
2 tsp Ginger and Garlic Paste (see page 17)
pinch of turmeric
1 green chili, chopped
½ tsp salt
1 tbsp butter
2–3 cloves garlic, chopped
2–3 whole dried chilies
½ tsp cumin seeds
¼ tsp Garnishing Garam Masala (see page 18)
1 tbsp chopped chives

FOOD VALUE

	TOTAL	PER PORTION (¼)
TOTAL FAT	14.3 g	3.6 g
SATURATED FAT	8.4 g	2.1 g
CHOLESTEROL	35 mg	9 mg
ENERGY (calories)	588	147

When served with rice, this meal is known as Dal Bhaat in India and Dal Chaval in Pakistan and is one of the most popular meals in both countries.

Rice and lentils is a traditional combination and an all-time favorite. The poor eat it because it is what they can afford, and the rich eat it because they happen to like the taste.

Do not be worried about the use of the whole dried chilies. When you are ready to serve, you can pick them out and use them for garnishing so your guests do not bite into them by mistake. They are worth trying as they lend the dish their own subtle flavor which cannot be achieved by using chili powder. If you do use chili powder instead, add it with the Ginger and Garlic Paste. *Never* use chili powder in the turka process, step 4, as it will burn and spoil the taste and color of the dish.

METHOD

1 The red lentils can be cooked without presoaking them, just put them into a medium-sized heavy-bottomed saucepan, wash them in 2 or 3 changes of water, then drain them.

2 Add 2½ cups of water, the Ginger and Garlic Paste, turmeric, green chili, and salt. Bring to a boil gradually over a medium heat, then lower the heat, cover, and simmer for 30 minutes.

3 Stir vigorously with a wooden spoon to help break up the lentils. Cook for about 10 more minutes, until the lentils have become soft and mushy – an indication that they are cooked and ready for the turka, the tempering of the dish, which you do next.

4 Melt the butter in a small skillet over a low heat. Add the garlic, whole dried chilies, and cumin seeds to the pan.

5 As soon as the seeds begin to sizzle, the chilies turn a shade darker, and the garlic pieces become pale pink, which will take about 2 minutes, pour the butter mixture over the lentils. Stir it well and simmer for another 2 to 3 minutes. Sprinkle the Garnishing Garam Masala and chives over the top just before serving. Take out the whole chilies before serving if you wish.

MALIKA MASOOR DAAL
Whole Brown Lentils
SERVES 4

INGREDIENTS

scant 1 cup brown lentils

2 tsp grated ginger root

a pinch turmeric

½ tsp salt

1 tbsp butter

2 tbsp chopped onion

3–4 cloves garlic, chopped

½ tsp cumin seeds

2–3 whole dried chilies (optional)
and ½ tsp chili powder

1–2 tbsp chopped cilantro leaves

FOOD VALUE

	TOTAL	PER PORTION (¼)
TOTAL FAT	15 7 g	3.9 g
SATURATED FAT	8.5 g	2.1 g
CHOLESTEROL	35 mg	9 mg
ENERGY (calories)	640	160

The word "Malika" means the Queen, and the humble brown lentil has been honored with this name because it is so popular. Underneath those turtle-brown shells lie the split red lentils that are more commonly seen in the West. Although the cooking methods for both lentils are similar, the taste and the look of the dish will vary a great deal. The brown lentil has an earthy taste of its own and makes a soft, brown, thick, soupy sauce.

METHOD

1 Pick over the lentils, then pour them into a medium-sized heavy-bottomed saucepan, wash them in a few changes of water, then soak them in 3 cups of water for 30 minutes.

2 Add the ginger, chili powder, turmeric, and salt and bring to a rapid boil. Reduce the heat and simmer for 30 minutes.

3 Although the lentils will be tender and soft at this stage, they will still have an insipid, watery look about them. Continue cooking and, at the same time, try to break or mash some of the lentils against the side of the saucepan with the back of a wooden spoon until the mixture takes on a thick, dissolved, and mushy look.

4 Melt the butter in a small skillet, add the onions and fry them until they begin to turn translucent.

5 Add the garlic, cumin seeds, and whole dried chilies if using any – it will take about 30 seconds for the garlic to turn pink. Then, add this sizzling mixture to the simmering lentils, stir, and leave it to simmer for another few minutes, and serve.

DAAL KE SHAMI KABOBS
Mung Bean Patties
SERVES 4

INGREDIENTS

4 oz dried mung beans
3 cloves
1 black cardamom pod, slit
½-inch piece cinnamon stick
2 tsp grated ginger root
2–3 cloves garlic, peeled
½ tsp chili powder
½ tsp salt
1 green chili, chopped
scant 1 cup mashed potato
½ tsp cumin seeds, crushed
3 tbsp cilantro leaves, chopped
2 tsp mint sauce
2 tsp lemon juice
2 scallions, chopped
2 tsp oil
1 large egg, beaten

FOOD VALUE

	TOTAL	PER PORTION (⅛)
TOTAL FAT	28.5 g	3.5 g
SATURATED FAT	4.4 g	0.5 g
CHOLESTEROL	181 mg	27 mg
ENERGY (calories)	663	84

Moong daal, or mung beans, are used here. If you cannot find split moong daal, you could use the whole kind, just soak and cook a bit longer.

METHOD

1 Rinse the mung beans in several changes of water, then soak them in 2½ cups of water for 1 hour so they soften and swell slightly. Then drain them off.

2 Pour 1 cup of fresh water into a heavy-bottomed saucepan, together with the cloves, black cardamom, cinnamon stick, ginger, garlic, chili powder, and salt. Cook the mung beans in this spiced water for 25 to 30 minutes, covered, over a medium heat or until the water disappears completely. To help quicken the evaporation, take the lid off during the last 10 minutes of cooking time. Stir occasionally to make sure they are not sticking to the bottom of the pan.

3 Once the liquid has evaporated, let the mung beans cool and discard the whole spices.

4 Grind the mung beans together with the green chili, roughly, in an electric blender.

5 Add the mashed potato, cumin seeds, and cilantro leaves to the bean mixture and blend them thoroughly.

6 Combine the mint sauce, lemon juice, scallion, and a pinch of salt in a small bowl, then put to one side. Now make the kabobs. Divide the mung bean mixture into 8 equal portions and form each portion into a ball. Make a little dent in the middle and put a little of the onion mixture into it. Cover the filling and flatten the ball into a burger shape.

7 Grease a large, nonstick skillet with half of the oil and heat it. Dip each kabob into the beaten egg and fry 4 of them first, gently turning them once only. They should be completely heated through, crispy, and golden brown. Use the remaining oil to cook the last 4 in the same way.

Mixed Masala Beans

SERVES 4

INGREDIENTS

1 tbsp oil
1/3 cup chopped onion
1/2 tsp cumin seeds
1/2 tsp chili powder
1/4 tsp turmeric
1/4 tsp Garam Masala (see page 18)
1 1/3 cups canned chick-peas, drained
1 1/3 cups canned kidney beans, drained
4 tbsp chopped tomatoes
1–2 green chilies, chopped
4 cloves garlic
1 tsp grated ginger root
2/3 cup chopped green bell pepper
2 tsp lemon juice
2–3 tbsp chopped cilantro leaves

FOOD VALUE

	TOTAL	PER PORTION (¼)
TOTAL FAT	19.3 g	4.8 g
SATURATED FAT	2.3 g	0.6 g
CHOLESTEROL	0	0
ENERGY (calories)	616	154

Not only do the ingredients blend well together, they also make a very colorful dish.

METHOD

1 Heat the oil in a medium-sized heavy-bottomed saucepan, then stir in the onion and cumin seeds and fry them until the onions turn a light gold color.

2 Add the chili powder, turmeric, and Garam Masala and stir. Add 2 tablespoons of water and cook, stirring continuously for 1 minute or so.

3 Gently stir in the chick-peas, kidney beans, tomato, green chilies, garlic, and ginger. Mix well and stir in 1 cup of water. Bring to a boil, then reduce the heat and simmer for 15 to 20 minutes.

4 Add the green pepper and cook for 2 to 3 minutes more.

5 Stir in the lemon juice and half the cilantro leaves. Use the remaining cilantro leaves to garnish the dish.

KABLI CHANNA
Chick-peas
SERVES 4

INGREDIENTS

2⅔ cups dried chick-peas

½ tsp baking soda

1 tsp salt

FOOD VALUE

	TOTAL	PER PORTION (¼)
TOTAL FAT	24.3 g	6.1 g
SATURATED FAT	2.3 g	0.6 g
CHOLESTEROL	0	0
ENERGY (calories)	1440	360

All the various celebrations and tea parties in Asian homes could never be the same without chick-peas. Although the thought of soaking them overnight and the lengthy cooking period is a bit offputting, they are so tasty and good for you that it is all worthwhile. Try the next few recipes to see how you feel.

Chick-peas are readily available canned and only need to be drained before using. They are about 40 calories per 1 ounce. They are convenient to have, but you can easily make large batches and freeze what you do not need straight away.

METHOD

1 Rinse the chick-peas and soak them overnight in 6¼ cups of water in a medium-sized heavy-bottomed saucepan.

2 Add the baking soda and salt and bring to a boil. Skim off the froth, cover the pan with a well-fitting lid, and simmer for 45 to 55 minutes, or until the chick-peas are absolutely tender yet retain their shape.

A cornucopia of nuts and pulses.

Spicy Chick-pea Salad

SERVES 4

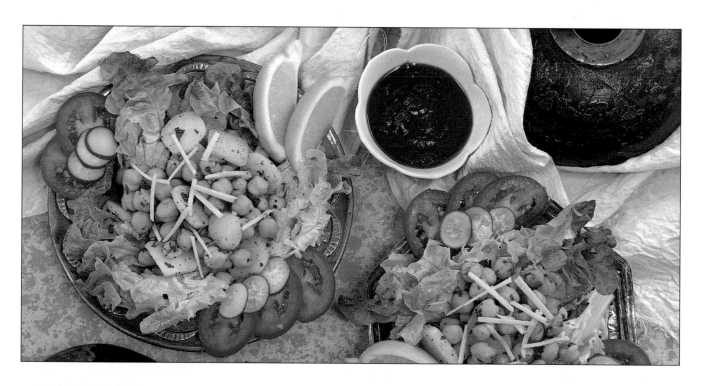

INGREDIENTS

1²⁄₃ canned chick-peas, drained
½ tsp chili powder
½ tsp cumin seeds, crushed
¼ tsp freshly ground black pepper
3 tbsp chopped cilantro and mint leaves
1 tsp juliennes of fresh ginger root
½ tsp coarse salt
½ pound boiled potatoes, cooled
4 oz lettuce
½ cup onion cut into thin rings
4 oz tomatoes, sliced
1 cup thinly sliced cucumber
4 oz radishes
wedges of lemon, to garnish
Tamarind Sauce (see page 16)

FOOD VALUE

	TOTAL	PER PORTION (¼)
TOTAL FAT	9.5 g	2.4 g
SATURATED FAT	1.1 g	0.3 g
CHOLESTEROL	0	0
ENERGY (calories)	557	139

Here canned chick-peas are used for sheer convenience. The best thing about the chick-peas is that they can be cooked without any oil.

METHOD

1 Put the chick-peas into a plastic container with a lid.

2 Sprinkle the chili powder, cumin seeds, freshly ground black pepper, half the cilantro and mint leaves, ginger, and the coarse salt on the chick-peas. Close the lid firmly and shake the container vigorously so the chick-peas become evenly coated with the herbs and spices and are even slightly bruised.

3 Dice the potato neatly or slice them thinly, then add them to the chick-peas, mix them in gently.

4 Make a bed of lettuce on each of 4 plates, spoon the spicy chick-pea salad onto the lettuce, scatter the remaining cilantro and mint leaves and ginger over the top. Surround with cucumber slices and chunks of radishes and sprinkle with lemon juice. Garnish with the onion and tomato and serve with wedges of lemon and lots of Tamarind Sauce.

Masala Chick-peas in Tamarind Sauce

SERVES 4

INGREDIENTS

4 tbsp chopped onion

¼ tsp turmeric

¼–½ tsp chili powder

2 tsp Ginger and Garlic Paste
(see page 17)

½ tsp coarse or ordinary salt

2⅔ cups chick-peas, cooked or canned,
drained

1 tbsp Tamarind Pulp (see page 16)

1 tsp artificial sugar

1–2 green chilies, chopped

4 oz tomatoes, sliced

¼ tsp Garam Masala (see page 18)

½ tsp cumin seeds, crushed

2 scallions, chopped

2–3 tbsp cilantro leaves

2 tsp lemon juice

FOOD VALUE

	TOTAL	PER PORTION (¼)
TOTAL FAT	10.1 g	2.5 g
SATURATED FAT	1 g	0.25 g
CHOLESTEROL	0	0
ENERGY (calories)	588	147

METHOD

1 Put the onion, turmeric, chili powder, Ginger and Garlic Paste and salt into a saucepan. Add 1 cup of water, bring to a boil, then reduce the heat and simmer for 5 minutes.

2 Stir in the chick-peas, Tamarind Pulp, sugar, green chilies, half the tomato, the Garam Masala and cumin seeds and cook for a few minutes.

3 Add ½ to ¾ cup of water, cover and simmer for 10 to 15 minutes.

4 In a separate container, mix the scallion, the rest of the tomato, the cilantro leaves and lemon juice. Use this mixture to garnish. Serve straight away or cold.

CHANNA SAAG
Broccoli with Chick-peas
SERVES 4

INGREDIENTS

½ cup sliced onion
2 tbsp oil
½ tsp cumin seeds
4 cloves garlic, finely chopped
½ tsp chili powder
¼ tsp turmeric
salt to taste
2½ cups chopped broccoli
⅓ cup chopped tomato
1⅓ cups canned chick-peas, drained
2 tsp grated ginger root
1 green chili, chopped
pinch of Garam Masala (see page 18)

FOOD VALUE

	TOTAL	PER PORTION (¼)
TOTAL FAT	32.1 g	8 g
SATURATED FAT	4.1 g	1 g
CHOLESTEROL	0	0
ENERGY (calories)	613	153

METHOD

1 Soften the onion in the oil in a medium-sized heavy-bottomed saucepan over a gentle heat.

2 Add the cumin seeds and garlic and cook for another minute or so.

3 Add the chili powder, turmeric, and salt and fry these spices well, adding a little water occasionally until the paste darkens slightly, which will take 2 to 3 minutes.

4 Add the broccoli and tomato, mix them in, cover the pan tightly and simmer gently for 20 minutes.

5 Gently stir in the chick-peas and add the ginger, green chili, and Garam Masala. Simmer for another 8 to 10 minutes before serving.

RAJMAH AUR IMLI
Kidney Beans in Tamarind Sauce
SERVES 4

INGREDIENTS

1 tbsp oil
⅓ cup chopped onion
½ tsp cumin seeds
1 tsp Ginger and Garlic Paste (see page 17)
½ tsp chili powder
a pinch turmeric
¼ tsp Garam Masala (see page 18)
¾ tsp salt
2⅔ cups canned kidney beans, well rinsed and drained
1 tbsp Tamarind Pulp (see page 16), or 2 tbsp lemon juice
1 tsp grated ginger root
1–2 green chilies, chopped
2 tbsp cilantro leaves or chopped chives, to garnish

FOOD VALUE

	TOTAL	PER PORTION (¼)
TOTAL FAT	14 g	3.5 g
SATURATED FAT	1.9 g	0.5 g
CHOLESTEROL	0	0
ENERGY (calories)	580	145

METHOD

1 Take a medium-sized heavy-bottomed saucepan and add the oil, onion, and cumin seeds and fry them until the onion changes color.

2 Add the Ginger and Garlic Paste, chili powder, turmeric, Garam Masala, and salt. Fry this mixture well for 1 to 2 minutes, adding a tiny amount of water, when necessary, to stop sticking or burning. As soon as the masala paste turns a shade darker, add the kidney beans and chopped tomatoes. Stir and cook for 2 to 3 minutes, until the beans have absorbed the flavor of the spices.

3 Pour in 1¼ cups of water, cover the pan, and simmer for 10 more minutes.

4 Add the Tamarind Pulp or lemon juice now, if using, together with the ginger and green chilies. Stir and cook for another 2 to 3 minutes.

5 Now, with a wooden spoon, mash a few beans against the side of the pan to thicken the sauce, then garnish with the cilantro leaves or chives.

Fresh vegetables are the essential basics of practically all Indian food.

RAJMAH
Kidney Beans in Thick, Spicy Sauce

SERVES 4

INGREDIENTS

1 cup dried kidney beans
salt to taste
½-inch piece of cinnamon stick
2–3 cloves
a pinch Garam Masala (see page 18)
1 tbsp oil
2 oz onion
1 tsp Ginger and Garlic Paste (see page 17)
¼ tsp turmeric
½ tsp chili powder
½ tsp grated ginger root
1–2 green chilies
2 tbsp cilantro leaves
2 tsp lemon juice
1 scallion, chopped

FOOD VALUE

	TOTAL	PER PORTION (¼)
TOTAL FAT	13.7 g	3.4 g
SATURATED FAT	1.7 g	0.4 g
CHOLESTEROL	0	0
ENERGY (calories)	587	147

See the information about cooking kidney beans on page 12 before starting this recipe.

METHOD

1 Wash and soak the beans for 3 to 4 hours in 5 cups of water.

2 Add the salt, the cinnamon stick, and cloves, cover and cook over a high heat for 30 minutes. Then reduce the heat and simmer for 40 more minutes.

3 Heat the oil in a small skillet and fry the onion until it turns golden brown.

4 Add the Ginger and Garlic Paste, turmeric, and chili powder. Cook the paste well, adding a little sprinkling of water at appropriate intervals to stop it from catching or burning and until it darkens slightly (this takes 2 to 3 minutes). Add this masala paste to the simmering beans and cook for 15 more minutes.

5 Add the grated ginger root, green chilies, and cilantro leaves.

6 The beans will be soft now so take a wooden spoon and mash a few against the side of the pan to thicken the sauce and give an appetizing, smooth, melting look to the beans. Mix the lemon juice with the scallion and use this to garnish the dish.

Kidney Beans in Thick, Spicy Sauce

LOBIA
Black-eyed Peas in Ginger and Tamarind Sauce
SERVES 4

INGREDIENTS

1 cup dried black-eyed beans

2 tsp grated ginger root

½ tsp chili powder

¼ tsp turmeric

½ tsp salt

1–2 green chilies (chopped)

1 tbsp Tamarind Pulp (see page 16)
or lowfat plain yogurt

1 tbsp oil

⅔ cup sliced onion

½ tsp cumin seeds

4–5 cloves garlic, chopped

¼ tsp Garam Masala (see page 18)

2–3 tbsp chopped cilantro leaves

FOOD VALUE

	TOTAL	PER PORTION (¼)
TOTAL FAT	14.4 g	3.6 g
SATURATED FAT	2.5 g	0.6 g
CHOLESTEROL	2 mg	0.5 mg
ENERGY (calories)	707	177

METHOD

1 Rinse and soak beans for a couple of hours in at least 3½ cups of water in a medium-sized saucepan.

2 Bring the beans to a boil over a medium heat, add half the ginger, the chili powder, turmeric, and salt, then reduce the heat, cover the pan and cook slowly for 45 to 50 minutes.

3 Add the remaining ginger, the green chilies, Tamarind Pulp or yogurt, mix it well and let it simmer for another 10 to 15 minutes.

4 In the meanwhile, heat the oil in a small skillet and fry the onion and, when it is about to color, add the cumin seeds and garlic. Remove the pan from the heat just as the garlic is turning golden brown.

5 Pour this mixture into the simmering beans, together with the Garam Masala. Stir and cook for another 5 minutes.

6 Just before serving, stir in the cilantro leaves and serve hot.

LOBIA SAAG
Black-eyed Peas and Broccoli
SERVES 4

INGREDIENTS

1 lb broccoli
⅓ cup chopped onion
2 tbsp oil
½ tsp cumin seeds
⅓ cup chopped tomato
½ tsp chili powder
1 tbsp lowfat plain yogurt
4–5 cloves garlic, chopped
2 cups canned black-eyed peas, drained
1 tsp grated ginger root
¼ tsp turmeric
a pinch Garam Masala (see page 18)
¾ tsp salt

FOOD VALUE

	TOTAL	PER PORTION (¼)
TOTAL FAT	29.3 g	7.3 g
SATURATED FAT	4.6 g	1.2 g
CHOLESTEROL	2 mg	0.5 mg
ENERGY (calories)	812	203

METHOD

1 Rinse and chop the broccoli into small flowerets, and chop the stems.

2 Fry the onion in the oil until it turns translucent, then add the cumin seeds and let them sizzle for 30 seconds.

3 Add the broccoli and tomato and cook, stirring continuously, for 1 minute or so.

4 Add the chili powder, yogurt, and garlic, mix them in and cook for 7 to 8 minutes over a low heat.

5 Add the black-eyed peas, ginger, turmeric, Garam Masala, and salt. Mix them in well and cook for 2 to 3 minutes.

6 Add ½ cup of water and bring to a boil, then reduce the heat and simmer for 10 to 15 minutes.

Curried Baked Beans

SERVES 2

INGREDIENTS

⅓ cup chopped onion

½ tsp cumin seeds, crushed

1 tbsp oil

¼ tsp chili powder

pinch of turmeric

2 cloves garlic or ¼ tsp garlic powder

1–2 green chilies (optional)

1⅓ cup baked beans

2 tsp lowfat plain yogurt

pinch Garam Masala (see page 18)

¼ tsp salt

cilantro leaves, mint leaves, or chives

FOOD VALUE

	TOTAL	PER PORTION (½)
TOTAL FAT	13.5 g	6.8 g
SATURATED FAT	1.9 g	1 g
CHOLESTEROL	1 mg	0.5 mg
ENERGY (calories)	429	214

This is an "emergency curry" for when the urge to eat something spicy catches you unprepared. If there's nothing in the refrigerator or freezer that can be turned into an instant curry, turn to the pantry and there you may find a couple of cans of baked beans and, hey presto, a few minutes later can enjoy a hot, spicy curry. My daughter says this recipe was very useful while she was at university.

METHOD

1 Fry the onion and cumin seeds in the oil in a saucepan. As soon as the onion turns translucent, add 1 tablespoon of water, then the chili powder, turmeric, garlic, and green chilies, if using.

2 Add another 2 tablespoons of water and cook this mixture for 2 to 3 minutes.

3 Add the baked beans, yogurt, Garam Masala, salt, and stir. Also add 4 tablespoons of hot water, cover and simmer for 2 to 3 minutes.

4 Stir in the lemon juice, cilantro or mint leaves or chives and remove from the heat.

PLAIN STEAMED RICE

LENTIL RICE

PILAU WITH PEAS

CHICK-PEA AND PEPPER PILAU

Rice Dishes

SHRIMP AND COCONUT PILAU

LENTILS AND RICE WITH FRIED ONIONS

RICE, LENTILS, AND VEGETABLE KHICHIRI

GARLIC KHICHIRI

MASALA RICE WITH POTATOES

MIXED VEGETABLE BIRYANI

LAMB OR BEEF BIRYANI

SPLIT PEA BIRYANI

SHRIMP AND MUSHROOM BIRYANI

LENTIL AND SHRIMP BIRYANI

Plain Steamed Rice

SERVES 4

INGREDIENTS

1 cup basmati or long-grain rice

1½ cups water

FOOD VALUE

	TOTAL	PER PORTION (¼)
TOTAL FAT	1 g	0.25 g
SATURATED FAT	Tr	Tr
CHOLESTEROL	0	0
ENERGY (calories)	718	180

METHOD

1 Wash the rice under running cold water and drain. Put it into a medium-sized heavy-bottomed saucepan with the measured water and let it soak for 10 to 15 minutes.

2 Bring it to a rapid boil over a medium heat, then reduce the heat so that the water is barely simmering. Cover the pan with a well-fitting lid that does not let out any steam and leave it to cook for about 15 minutes. It is important that you suppress any temptation to lift the lid to take a peek during this time because the valuable steam will escape, hindering the cooking process.

Lentil Rice

SERVES 4

INGREDIENTS

scant 1 cup basmati or long-grain rice

1⅔ cups red lentils

1½ cups water

FOOD VALUE

	TOTAL	PER PORTION (¼)
TOTAL FAT	1.2 g	0.3 g
SATURATED FAT	Tr	Tr
CHOLESTEROL	0	0
ENERGY (calories)	708	177

This is not a traditional lentil and rice Khichiri because it would normally be cooked with fried onions and whole spices.

METHOD

1 Combine the rice with the red lentils and wash and drain them well. Put both into a medium-sized heavy-bottomed saucepan.

2 Pour in the fresh water and soak for 10 to 15 minutes.

3 Over a medium heat, bring it to a boil, then, straight away, reduce the heat, cover the pan with a well-fitting lid and leave it to simmer gently for about 15 minutes. Do *not* lift the lid during this time.

4 Switch off the heat and leave the pan to stand for 2 to 3 minutes to let the steam work its final magic.

MUTTER PILLAU
Pilau with Peas
SERVES 4

INGREDIENTS

heaped 1 cup rice
½ cup sliced onion
2 tbsp oil
2–3 cloves
½-inch piece cinnamon stick
1 brown cardamom pod, slit or bruised
1 tsp cumin seeds
scant 1 cup frozen peas
1 tsp salt

FOOD VALUE

	TOTAL	PER PORTION (¼)
TOTAL FAT	24.8 g	6.2 g
SATURATED FAT	2.9 g	0.7 g
CHOLESTEROL	0	0
ENERGY (calories)	1116	279

METHOD

1 Wash and soak the rice for 20 minutes, then drain it well and put it to one side.

2 Fry the onion in the oil in a heavy-bottomed saucepan. Add the cloves, cinnamon stick, and cardamom pod and cook until the onions become a rich brown color.

3 Add 1¾ cups of water and let it come to a boil.

4 Add the rice and peas at this stage, stir in the salt and reduce the heat so it is just simmering. Cover the pan with a well-fitting lid and cook for 20 minutes. Let it stand for 2 to 3 minutes before serving.

Opposite:
Paddy fields in the south of India.

Chick-pea and Pepper Pilau

SERVES 4

INGREDIENTS

1 cup basmati or long-grain rice
2 tbsp oil
2 oz onion
½-inch piece cinnamon stick
3 cloves
1 black cardamom pod, slit or bruised
2–3 bay leaves
½ tsp cumin seeds
1 cup cooked or canned chick-peas, drained
¾ tsp salt
½ cup chopped red and green bell peppers
3–4 cloves garlic, chopped

FOOD VALUE

	TOTAL	PER PORTION (¼)
TOTAL FAT	28.7 g	7.2 g
SATURATED FAT	3.1 g	0.8 g
CHOLESTEROL	0	0
ENERGY (calories)	1125	281

The mixture of red and green peppers makes this dish wonderfully colorful.

METHOD

1 Wash the rice, then soak it for 15 to 20 minutes. Drain it well and keep it to one side.

2 Heat the oil in a medium-sized heavy-bottomed saucepan and fry the onion together with the cinnamon stick, cloves, cardamom pod, bay leaves, and cumin seeds until the onion turns a rich golden color.

3 Add 1½ cups of water and bring it to a boil.

4 As soon as the water begins to bubble, add the rice, chick-peas, and salt, cover the pan with a well-fitting lid and simmer for 12 to 15 minutes.

5 Mix in the peppers and garlic gently with a fork, then cover again and let it steam for another 2 to 3 minutes. Let is stand for a few minutes before serving.

Shrimp and Coconut Pilau

SERVES 4

INGREDIENTS

3 oz onion
2 tbsp oil
1 tsp cumin seeds
3 cloves
½-inch piece cinnamon stick
1 black cardamom pod, slit or bruised
3 cloves garlic, chopped
1 tsp grated ginger root
1 tbsp shredded coconut
½ tsp salt
6 ounces shrimp
1 tbsp lowfat plain yogurt
heaped 1 cup basmati or long-grain rice

FOOD VALUE

	TOTAL	PER PORTION (¼)
TOTAL FAT	36.2 g	9 g
SATURATED FAT	11.7 g	2.9 g
CHOLESTEROL	144 mg	36 mg
ENERGY (calories)	1338	335

METHOD

1 Fry the onions in the oil in a medium-sized heavy-bottomed saucepan, adding the cumin, cloves, cinnamon stick, and cardamom pod, cooking until the onion turns a rich golden color.

2 Add the garlic, ginger, coconut, and salt and cook these together for a few seconds.

3 Add the shrimp and yogurt, mix well and cook for another minute.

4 Add the rice and stir it in. Pour in 1¾ cups of water, cover the pan and simmer for 20 minutes. Let it stand for another 2 to 3 minutes before serving.

Shrimp and Coconut Pilau.

CHANNA DAAL KHICHIRI
Lentils and Rice with Fried Onions
SERVES 4

INGREDIENTS

1 cup rice
⅓ cup lentils
½ cup sliced onion
1 tbsp oil
1 tsp cumin seeds
½-inch piece cinnamon stick
2 cloves
1 brown cardamom pod, slit or bruised
10–12 peppercorns (optional)
½ tsp salt

FOOD VALUE

	TOTAL	PER PORTION (¼)
TOTAL FAT	28.5 g	7.1 g
SATURATED FAT	3.4 g	0.9 g
CHOLESTEROL	0	0
ENERGY (calories)	1173	293

Khichiri is an all-in-one convenient and very popular rice meal in India and Pakistan. The same dish made its name as Kedgeree in the West in the Victorian era and, for some reason, it was known as a breakfast dish, with the difference that fish is added to the dish instead of lentils.

Lentils are always an important ingredient of Khichiri – without them this rice dish would be a simple pilau or Bhugarey chavel or, perhaps, plain fried rice.

There are quite a few varieties of Khichiri. Essentially a rice and lentil dish, vegetables are sometimes added.

METHOD

1 Rinse the rice and lentils separately, then soak them in 2½ cups of water for 20 to 25 minutes. Drain them well, then put them to one side.

2 Fry the onions in the oil in a heavy-bottomed saucepan, together with the cumin seeds, cinnamon stick, cloves, cardamom pod, and peppercorns until the onions turn a deep, rich golden brown. (Here the fried onions also act as a dye – the browner the onions, the richer the color they will turn the rice.)

3 Add 2¼ cups of water and put in the lentils first; let it come to a boil, reduce heat to a minimum, and cover and cook for 10 minutes. Add the drained rice and salt, stirring gently to mix the lentils and rice together. Cover and continue to cook for 20 to 25 minutes. Let it stand for 3 to 4 minutes before serving.

Delightful painted patterns and colors are found on many buildings throughout India, and this love of diversity is seen in the country's cuisine, too. The rich variety of life is apparent everywhere.

SUBZI AUR MASALA KHICHIRI
Rice, Lentil, and Vegetable Khichiri
SERVES 4

INGREDIENTS

⅓ cup red lentils
1 cup basmati or long-grain rice
½ cup chopped onion
½-inch piece cinnamon stick
2–3 cloves
1 black cardamom pod, slit or bruised (optional)
1 tsp cumin seeds
2 tbsp oil
¼ tsp turmeric
½ tsp chili powder
1 tsp salt
2 tsp Ginger and Garlic Paste (see page 17)
1 tbsp lowfat plain yogurt
½ cup chopped green beans
½ cup diced carrot
4 tbsp chopped tomato

FOOD VALUE

	TOTAL	PER PORTION (¼)
TOTAL FAT	25 g	6.2 g
SATURATED FAT	3.2 g	0.8 g
CHOLESTEROL	2 mg	0.5 mg
ENERGY (calories)	1182	296

METHOD

1 Rinse lentils and rice together, then soak them in 2½ cups of water for 15 to 20 minutes. Then drain them well and keep to one side.

2 Fry the onion, cinnamon stick, cloves, cardamom pod, if using, and cumin seeds in the oil in a medium-sized heavy-bottomed saucepan.

3 As the onion turns a deep golden color, add the turmeric, chili powder, salt, Ginger and Garlic Paste, and the yogurt and fry this masala mixture, adding a little water at a time for 2 to 3 minutes.

4 Add the green beans, carrot, and tomato, mix and cook for 1 minute or so. Add the rice and lentil mixture, stir to blend, then add scant 2 cups of water, cover the pan with a tight-fitting lid, and bring it to a boil. Reduce the heat and simmer for 20 minutes, then let it stand for 3 to 4 minutes before serving.

LUSSAN KI KHICHIRI
Garlic Khichiri
SERVES 4

INGREDIENTS

¼ cup dried mung beans

1 cup basmati or long-grain rice

6–7 plump cloves garlic, chopped or crushed

2 tbsp chopped chives

1 tsp lemon juice

2 tbsp oil

½ cup sliced onion

1 tbsp yogurt

2–3 cloves

½-inch piece cinnamon stick

½ tsp cumin seeds

½ tsp salt

FOOD VALUE

	TOTAL	PER PORTION (¼)
TOTAL FAT	24.2 g	6 g
SATURATED FAT	3 g	0.8 g
CHOLESTEROL	2 mg	0.5 mg
ENERGY (calories)	1130	283

METHOD

1 Rinse the mung beans and rice together and soak them for 15 to 20 minutes. Then drain them well and put them to one side.

2 Mix the garlic with chives and lemon juice in a small bowl and keep this mixture to one side.

3 Heat the oil in a medium-sized heavy-bottomed saucepan and add the onion, cloves, cinnamon stick, and cumin seeds. Fry until the onion is a rich, golden color and then stir in the yogurt.

4 Add scant 2 cups of water and the salt. As soon as the water comes to a boil, add the rice and mung bean mixture, reduce the heat, cover with a well-fitting lid and simmer for 10 to 12 minutes.

5 Make 2 or 3 deep dents in the surface of the rice with a tablespoon and gently drop the garlic and chive mixture into them, then cover it up with the rice. Cook, covered, for a further 7 to 8 minutes. Let the dish stand for a few minutes before serving.

TAHIRI
Masala Rice with Potatoes
SERVES 4

INGREDIENTS

½ lb potatoes

heaped 1 cup basmati or long-grain rice

2 tbsp oil

½ cup chopped onion

2–3 cloves

½-inch piece cinnamon stick

1 black cardamom pod, bruised or slit

2 or 3 bay leaves

½ tsp cumin seeds

2 tsp Ginger and Garlic Paste
(see page 17)

¼ tsp turmeric

½ tsp chili powder

¾ tsp salt

1 tbsp lowfat plain yogurt

1 green chili, chopped

FOOD VALUE

	TOTAL	PER PORTION (¼)
TOTAL FAT	24.2 g	6.1 g
SATURATED FAT	2.9 g	0.7 g
CHOLESTEROL	2 mg	0.5 mg
ENERGY (calories)	1230	307

This has been one of my favorite rice dishes ever since school days. I loved it so much I was convinced I could live on it for the rest of my life! At home we ate it with mint and raw mango or fresh cilantro and garlic sauce and a special raita made with tiny chick-pea flour dumplings. Every time I ate it, I thought I was in heaven!

METHOD

1 Scrub the potatoes well, but do not peel them. Cut them into eighths.

2 Rinse and soak the rice for 10 to 15 minutes, then drain it well and keep it to one side.

3 Heat the oil in a medium-sized heavy-bottomed saucepan, add the onion, the cloves, cinnamon stick, cardamom pod, and cumin seeds and fry until the onion turns a rich golden color.

4 Add the Ginger and Garlic Paste, turmeric, chili powder, and salt. Stir and cook the spices well, then add the yogurt and 1 tablespoon of water to prevent it sticking and burning.

5 Add scant 2 cups of water, let it come to a boil, then add the rice, potatoes, and green chili. Cover the pan tightly and simmer for about 25 minutes. Then let it stand for another 3 to 4 minutes before serving.

SUBZI KI BIRYANI
Mixed Vegetable Biryani
SERVES 4

INGREDIENTS

heaped 1 cup basmati rice

3 oz button mushrooms

3 oz green beans

2 tbsp lowfat plain yogurt

3 tbsp oil

2/3 cup chopped onion

1/2 tsp Roasted and Crushed Cumin Seeds (see page 17)

1/4 tsp black cumin seeds (optional)

3–4 cloves garlic, chopped or crushed

2 tsp grated ginger root

1/4 tsp turmeric

1/2 tsp chili powder

1/2 tsp salt

1/2 cup chopped red bell pepper

1/3 cup frozen peas

1/3 cup chopped tomato

2 green chilies, chopped

a pinch grated mace

1 tbsp sterilized cream

2 tbsp mint or cilantro leaves, chopped

3 cloves

1/2-inch piece cinnamon stick

3 or 4 green cardamom pods, slit

2 or 3 bay leaves

FOOD VALUE

	TOTAL	PER PORTION (1/4)
TOTAL FAT	40 g	10 g
SATURATED FAT	6.6 g	1.6 g
CHOLESTEROL	12 mg	3 mg
ENERGY (calories)	1334	334

METHOD

1 Rinse the rice, soak it for 15 to 20 minutes, then drain it well.

2 Wipe the mushrooms clean and slice the large ones into halves or quarters, leaving the tiny ones whole.

3 Rinse, top and tail, and string the beans, then cut them into 1/2-inch pieces.

4 Dilute the yogurt with 3 to 4 tablespoons of water and keep this mixture to one side.

5 Heat one-third of the oil in a medium-sized heavy-bottomed saucepan and fry the onion and Cumin Seeds together. As soon as the onions turn a golden color, lift them out and put them in a strainer, pressing them with a wooden spoon to squeeze the oil back into the saucepan.

6 Add the remaining oil to the same pan, and as it heats up, add the black cumin seeds, if using, garlic, and ginger and let them sizzle for 30 seconds.

7 Add the turmeric, chili powder, and salt. Cook the spices together, stirring continuously, for another minute or so.

8 Now add the mushrooms, red peppers, green beans, peas, tomato, and green chilies. Stir to mix them in well, then cover the pan and simmer for 8 to 10 minutes. Increase heat to medium, remove the lid and, stirring occasionally, cook until the moisture has evaporated and the curry appears to be fairly dry and add the mace. (Too much moisture will run through the rice layers later and will ruin your biryani.)

9 Spoon in the cream and mint or cilantro leaves, reserving some for garnishing, mix gently and remove the pan from the heat.

10 Add the cloves, cinnamon stick, cardamom pods, bay leaves, and a pinch of salt to a medium-sized heavy-bottomed saucepan together with 5 cups of water and bring it to a boil on high heat. As it begins to bubble, add the rice and let it cook in rapidly boiling water for just 2 minutes – be strict about this as the rice must be only parboiled at this stage. Drain it well and rinse out the pan.

11 Transfer the rice to a large platter, discarding the whole spices. Add the fried onion and cumin mixture to it, mixing gently with a fork, then divide the mixture into three equal piles.

12 Take your cleaned saucepan and spread the first pile of rice evenly over the bottom. Spoon half the vegetable mixture evenly over the bed of rice. Cover the vegetable mixture with the second pile of rice, again spreading it evenly. Repeat the last 2 steps, then garnish the top with the reserved mint or cilantro leaves. Pour the diluted yogurt evenly over the rice. Cover the pan with a well-fitting lid and simmer gently for 20 to 25 minutes, or until the rice is tender.

Lamb or Beef Biryani

SERVES 4

heaped 1 cup basmati rice

*½ pound lean lamb or beef
(leg of lamb or braising steak)*

3 tbsp lowfat plain yogurt

½ tsp black cumin seeds (optional)

½ tsp chili powder

½ tsp Garam Masala (see page 18)

*2 tbsp Ginger and Garlic Paste
(see page 17)*

1 tsp salt (optional)

¼ tsp saffron

3 tbsp skim milk, hot

3 tbsp oil

⅔ cup chopped onion

5 green cardamom pods, bruised or slit

2 black cardamom pods, bruised or slit

4 cloves

2 green chilies, chopped

2 tsp lemon juice

a pinch freshly grated mace

½-inch piece cinnamon stick

2 or 3 bay leaves

½ tsp cumin seeds, crushed

2 tbsp cilantro leaves

FOOD VALUE

	TOTAL	PER PORTION (¼)
TOTAL FAT	55.3 g	13.8 g
SATURATED FAT	14.2 g	3.5 g
CHOLESTEROL	184 mg	46 mg
ENERGY (calories)	1590	398

Biryanis are some of the richest and most exotic dishes in the Indian cook's repertoire. Milk, cream, nuts, and dry fruits, the inclusion of anything is possible! The following recipes are a few simple, rather innocent versions of this dish – far less sinful caloriewise, but enormously pleasing in taste and flavor. You will have to agree that, no matter what, a biryani is a biryani and, as such, is unquestionably one of the true queens of all rice dishes.

Biryanis are famous for their richness, but, here, my aim has been to limit the calories to no more than 400. You should not need to add much in terms of accompaniments either, so you can save calories here, too. All they need, at the most, is a cool, simple raita, lightly garnished with some crunchy vegetables, or any of the meat, fish, or vegetable kabobs.

When serving a biryani from the saucepan, stab the serving spoon into it, piercing it all the way down to the bottom of the pan so that it cuts through the layers very much like a cake, then lift out all three layers and gently spread the rice, very much like opening a Japanese fan, from the center to the edge of the serving dish.

I recommend that you use only the basmati rice when making biryani. If you put the very best of everything you have into this dish you will be richly rewarded.

METHOD

1 Rinse the rice, soak for 20 to 25 minutes, and drain it very well.

2 Rinse and cut the lamb or beef into cubes not bigger than 1 inch.

3 Mix the yogurt with the black cumin seeds, if using, chili powder, Garam Masala, Ginger and Garlic Paste, and salt in a small bowl and marinate the lamb or beef pieces in it.

4 If using saffron, heat a small skillet. Place the saffron strands in it and switch the heat off. Stir them with a wooden spoon while the pan is hot, then leave them there to cool. This makes them crispy and easy to crush. Crush them into a powder with the tips of your fingers and add it to the hot milk, leaving it to infuse.

5 Heat the oil in a medium-sized heavy-bottomed saucepan, then add the onion, green and black cardamom pods, and cloves. Fry gently until the onion becomes a rich golden brown. Lift most but not all the fried onions, pressing them against the sides of the pan to let as much oil drip back into the pan as possible. Keep these onions to one side.

6 Drop the marinated meat into the same saucepan and stir-fry it quickly, adding about 1 tablespoon of water from time to time, cooking for at least 2 to 3 minutes over a medium heat.

7 Add the green chilies, lemon juice and mace, reduce the heat, cover with a well-fitting lid and simmer for 15 to 20 minutes, or until the moisture has been absorbed and the sauce is fairly dry.

8 While the meat is cooking, put the rice into another medium-sized heavy-bottomed saucepan with 5 cups of water, together with the cinnamon stick, bay leaves, and a pinch of salt. It is important at this stage that the rice is only parboiled, so keep a careful eye on it and, once the water begins to bubble rapidly, allow the rice to cook for just 2 minutes, then drain it very well. Rinse out the pan.

9 Break or crush the reserved fried onions and mix them with the cumin seeds, then add this mixture to the parboiled rice, mixing it in with a fork, and picking out and discarding the whole spices at the same time. Divide the rice into 3 equal piles on a platter and keep it to one side.

10 Using the same saucepan in which you prepared the rice, spread 1 of the piles of rice over the bottom of the pan. Spoon half the meat mixture over the rice, spreading it evenly. Dot the top with the cilantro leaves. Cover the meat mixture with the second pile of rice. Repeat the last 2 steps again.

Finally, pour the saffron milk evenly over the rice, covering its entire surface. Cover the pan with a tight-fitting lid and simmer for 20 to 25 minutes, or until the rice has cooked through.

Split Pea Biryani

SERVES 4

INGREDIENTS

1 heaped cup basmati or long-grain rice

⅔ cup yellow split peas

3–4 green cardamom pods, slit or bruised

1 black cardamom pod, slit or bruised

½-inch piece cinnamon stick

2 or 3 bay leaves

1 tsp salt

scant 1 cup finely sliced onion

3 tbsp oil

4 cloves

½ tsp cumin seeds

pinch of turmeric

½ tsp chili powder

¼ tsp Garam Masala (see page 18)

1 tsp Ginger and Garlic Paste (see page 17)

2 tbsp lowfat plain yogurt

pinch of grated nutmeg

2 green chilies, chopped

1 tsp grated ginger root

4 tbsp chopped cilantro leaves

2 tsp lemon juice

mint, to garnish

FOOD VALUE

	TOTAL	PER PORTION (¼)
TOTAL FAT	41.7 g	10.4 g
SATURATED FAT	6.1 g	1.5 g
CHOLESTEROL	11 mg	3 mg
ENERGY (calories)	1579	395

I have used yellow split peas for this biryani as it is wholesome and grainy, lending a lovely texture to this dish.

METHOD

1 Rinse the rice and the split peas separately and soak each for 20 to 25 minutes. Then, drain them very well and keep them to one side.

2 Add the green and black cardamom pods, cinnamon stick, bay leaves, and a little salt into 5 cups of water in a medium-sized heavy-bottomed saucepan and bring to a boil, gradually. Add the rice and parboil by letting it cook in rapidly boiling water for just 2 minutes. It is important that the rice is not allowed to cook completely at this stage. Drain it off thoroughly and keep it to one side. Rinse out the pan for use later.

3 Fry the onions in the oil over a medium heat until they are a deep golden color in places. Spoon most of them out, pressing the spoon well against the side of the pan, draining as much oil back into the pan as possible and keep these to one side.

4 To the remaining few onions in the pan, add the cloves and cumin seeds and stir-fry for 30 seconds.

5 Add the turmeric, chili powder, Garam Masala, Ginger and Garlic Paste, and salt. Fry these spices well, adding a little water, when necessary to stop the mixture sticking, and stirring continuously.

6 Add the split peas and 1¼ cups of hot water, stir, cover, and simmer for 25 to 30 minutes, or until the split peas are almost cooked.

7 Add the yogurt and nutmeg and cook until the excess moisture has completely evaporated and the split peas are absolutely tender, but each one retains its shape.

8 Mix in the green chilies, ginger, and half the cilantro leaves. Mix well and remove pan from heat.

9 Add the reserved fried onions to the parboiled rice (keeping just a few of them to one side to garnish later) mixing them gently into the rice with a fork, picking out the whole spices as you do so.

10 In your rinsed saucepan, spread half the onion rice in an even layer over the bottom. Spread all the lentil mixture evenly over the rice, then sprinkle the remaining cilantro leaves over the top, squeeze the lemon juice over the top, then spread the remaining rice mixture over the split pleas and cilantro, covering them completely.

11 Garnish the top with the reserved fried onions and the mint or other green herb, if using. Sprinkle 3 to 4 tablespoons of hot water (if the lentils are too dry, add a little more liquid) over the rice, cover the pan with a well-fitting lid, and simmer gently for 20 to 25 minutes, or until the rice is cooked.

Shrimp and Mushroom Biryani

SERVES 4

INGREDIENTS

heaped 1 cup rice
½ lb shelled shrimp
3 oz button mushrooms
3 tbsp oil
15 fenugreek seeds
2 tsp Ginger and Garlic Paste (see page 17)
2 tbsp lowfat plain yogurt
¼ tsp turmeric
a pinch of freshly grated mace
½ tsp chili powder
1 tsp salt
1 green chili, chopped
2 tsp lemon juice
3 tbsp chopped cilantro leaves
2 cloves
½-inch piece cinnamon stick
2 bay leaves
2–3 green cardamom pods, slit or bruised
¼ tsp cumin seeds, crushed
3 tbsp skim milk
2 scallions, chopped

FOOD VALUE

	TOTAL	PER PORTION (¼)
TOTAL FAT	40 g	10 g
SATURATED FAT	5.7 g	1.4 g
CHOLESTEROL	186 mg	47 mg
ENERGY (calories)	1421	355

METHOD

1 Rinse and then soak the rice for 15 to 20 minutes. Drain it very well and keep it to one side.

2 Rinse and pat the shrimp dry.

3 Wipe the mushrooms clean.

4 Heat the oil in a medium-sized heavy-bottomed saucepan, add the fenugreek seeds, stir-fry them for 30 seconds then add the Ginger and Garlic Paste, yogurt, turmeric, chili powder, and salt. Mix and cook until the spices darken a little (this should take 1–2 minutes), sprinkling a little water over it if need be, to prevent it burning or sticking.

5 Add the shrimp and cook them for 30 seconds.

6 Stir in the mushrooms, green chili and mace until everything is well mixed together, then cover the pan and let it simmer for 5 minutes.

7 Remove the lid, increase the heat slightly, and evaporate the excess moisture, stirring all the time.

8 Add the lemon juice and half the cilantro leaves, give the mixture a final stir and then set it to one side.

9 Add the remaining salt and the cloves, cinnamon stick, bay leaves, and cardamom pods to 5 cups of water in a medium-sized heavy-bottomed saucepan and bring it to a boil gradually over a medium heat. As soon as it begins to bubble, add the rice and boil it for just 2 minutes. Watch the time carefully as it is important to only cook it partially at this stage, then drain it very well and pick out the whole spices. Mix the remaining cilantro leaves and cumin seeds gently into the rice with a fork and spoon it into 3 equal-sized piles on a platter. Rinse out the pan to use next.

10 Swirl the skim milk to cover the bottom of the pan. Spread the first pile of rice evenly over the bottom of the pan, then spoon half the shrimp and mushroom mixture over the rice to form an even layer. Repeat these last 2 layers and top with the remaining rice. Garnish it with the scallion and then sprinkle 3 to 4 tablespoons of hot water evenly over the top, cover with a well-fitting lid, and simmer gently for 20 to 25 minutes.

DAAL AUR JHINGA BIRYANI
Lentil and Shrimp Biryani
SERVES 4

INGREDIENTS

⅓ cup brown lentils
1 cup basmati rice
2 tbsp oil
12 fenugreek seeds
½ tsp cumin seeds
¼ tsp mustard seeds
2 tsp Ginger and Garlic Paste (see page 17)
½ tsp chili powder
¼ tsp turmeric
½ tsp salt
½ pound shelled shrimp
1 tbsp lowfat plain yogurt
1–2 green chilies
1 tsp grated ginger root
2 tsp lemon juice
3 or 4 green cardamom pods, slit
2 or 3 bay leaves
3 cloves
½-inch piece cinnamon stick
1 scallion, chopped

FOOD VALUE

	TOTAL	PER PORTION (¼)
TOTAL FAT	25.9 g	6.5 g
SATURATED FAT	3.1 g	0.8 g
CHOLESTEROL	352 mg	88 mg
ENERGY (calories)	1224	306

Brown lentils make the biryani nicely grainy so it keeps its shape and does not disintegrate. It is delicious and the turtle-colored grains look exceptionally pretty.

METHOD

1 Rinse the lentils and rice separately, soak them in separate containers for 20 minutes, then drain the rice very well.

2 Drain the lentils, then transfer them to a medium-sized heavy-bottomed saucepan and pour in ¾ cup of fresh water.

3 Heat the oil in a medium-sized heavy-bottomed saucepan, add the fenugreek, mustard, and cumin seeds and let them sizzle for a minute.

4 Add the Ginger and Garlic Paste, chili powder, turmeric, and salt and fry this mixture, stirring, for a good minute until the spices turn a slightly darker shade, adding a sprinkling of water, if necessary, to prevent the paste sticking or burning.

5 Add the shrimp, mix them in well, then stir in the yogurt and cook the mixture briefly over a medium heat, then lower the heat, add half the green chilies and cook for another couple of minutes, making sure that the moisture has evaporated.

6 Cook the lentils over a low heat, adding the ginger, remaining green chilies, and a pinch of salt, until the moisture has completely evaporated. The lentils should be soft but not mushy; it is important that they should retain their shape. Stir in the lemon juice.

7 Add the cardamom pods, bay leaves, cloves, cinnamon stick, and a pinch of salt to 5 cups of water and bring it to a boil. As soon as it bubbles, pour in the rice with a pinch of salt and let it cook for no more than 3 to 4 minutes. (Measure the time exactly as it must only cook partially at this stage.) Drain well.

8 Combine the lentils with the rice, discarding the spices as you find them. Mix in the cilantro leaves gently with a fork, reserving some for garnishing later. Spoon the rice into 3 equal piles on a large platter or tray and rinse the pan to use next.

9 Spread the first pile of rice mixture evenly over the bottom of the cleaned pan. Spoon half the shrimp mixture evenly over the rice, dotting some of the scallion over it. Repeat these last 2 steps, then spread the remaining rice mixture over the top, garnishing with the cilantro leaves or remaining scallion. Sprinkle 3 to 4 tablespoons of hot water evenly over the top, cover with a well-fitting lid, and simmer gently for about 20 to 25 minutes, or until the rice is thoroughly cooked, adding a little more hot water, if it has become too dry and cook for a little longer.

UNDAY AUR MUTTER KA SALAN
Egg and Peas Curry
SERVES 4

INGREDIENTS

4 large eggs

2 tbsp oil

1/3 cup chopped onion

1/4 tsp cumin seeds

2 tsp Ginger and Garlic Paste
(see page 17)

1/2 tsp chili powder

1/4 tsp turmeric

1/2 tsp ground coriander

salt to taste

1/4 tsp Garam Masala (see page 18)

1/3 cup chopped tomato

scant 1 cup fresh or frozen peas

1 green chili, slit

2 tbsp cilantro leaves

FOOD VALUE

	TOTAL	PER PORTION (1/4)
TOTAL FAT	58.3 g	14.6 g
SATURATED FAT	12.9 g	3.2 g
CHOLESTEROL	1232 mg	308 mg
ENERGY (calories)	783	196

METHOD

1 Hard-boil the eggs, remove their shells, then keep them to one side.

2 Heat the oil in a medium-sized heavy-bottomed saucepan and fry the onion and cumin seeds until the onion is light gold in color.

3 Add the Ginger and Garlic Paste, chili powder, turmeric, ground coriander, salt, and Garam Masala and fry this mixture well for a couple of minutes, adding, whenever needed, 1 tablespoon of water, to prevent it burning or sticking.

4 Add the whole eggs and tomato, stir gently and cook for a minute.

5 Add 1¼ cups of water and let it come to a boil before adding the peas and green chili. Cook for another 5 minutes.

6 Stir in the cilantro leaves and remove the pan from the heat.

LUSSAN AUR MIRACH KA OMELETTE
Chili and Garlic Omelet
SERVES 2

INGREDIENTS

3 large eggs

1 green chili, chopped

2–3 garlic cloves, chopped or crushed

⅓ cup chopped onion

1–2 tbsp cilantro leaves or chopped fresh chives

good pinch of chili powder

¼ tsp cumin seeds

salt to taste

2 tbsp skim milk

2 tsp oil

FOOD VALUE

	TOTAL	PER PORTION (½)
TOTAL FAT	24.6 g	12.3 g
SATURATED FAT	6 g	3 g
CHOLESTEROL	658 mg	329 mg
ENERGY (calories)	323	162

Even after so many years living in England, I still enjoy a chili omelet for Sunday brunch. Many of my English friends have tried this (with parathas, pooris, or toast) and they love it, too.

Even if you can't afford the luxury of a paratha (a fried Indian bread), which, because it is fried, contains quite a few calories, there is nothing to stop you enjoying this omelet with a chapati, pita bread, or toasted brown bread. The best part is that this dish is very quick and easy to prepare.

METHOD

1 Break the eggs into a bowl and beat until they are slightly frothy.

2 Add the green chili, garlic, onion, cilantro leaves or chives, chili powder, cumin seeds, and salt, together with the milk and beat a bit more to mix the herbs and spices well together.

3 Grease a nonstick skillet with the oil and heat it to smoking point.

4 Pour in the egg mixture and reduce the heat. You can then choose to keep the omelet whole, turning it quickly to cook the other side when the first is done, to fold it and divide it into 2 portions or to make scrambled eggs, stirring and breaking the egg mixture while it is cooking. All of these methods are used in our house to please everyone in the family and all taste good.

Egg and Potato Omelet
SERVES 2

INGREDIENTS

3 large eggs

4 oz potatoes

2 scallions

¼ tsp chili powder

3 cloves garlic, chopped

½ tsp salt

1 tbsp oil

½ tsp grated ginger root

¼ tsp cumin seeds, crushed

2 tbsp chopped cilantro leaves

FOOD VALUE

	TOTAL	PER PORTION (½)
TOTAL FAT	30 g	15 g
SATURATED FAT	6.6 g	3.3 g
CHOLESTEROL	658 mg	329 mg
ENERGY (calories)	434	217

METHOD

1 Break the eggs into a bowl and beat until they are foaming.

2 Scrub the potatoes, leaving the skins on, then finely dice or slice them.

3 Wipe and chop the scallions.

4 Mix the chili powder, garlic, and half the salt into the eggs.

5 Grease a nonstick pan with the oil and fry the ginger and cumin seeds for 1 minute.

6 Add the potato and stir-fry it for 1 minute.

7 Add the salt and 2 tablespoons of water, cover, and cook over a low heat for 6 to 7 minutes, or until the potatoes are almost done, adding a little more water, if need be.

8 Scatter the cilantro leaves over the potato mixture and do not stir. Immediately, pour in the egg mixture. Cook until it is firm, finish it under a hot broiler. Serve immediately.

Mushroom Masala Omelet

SERVES 2

INGREDIENTS

3 large eggs
1 tsp all-purpose flour
2 tbsp chopped green or red bell pepper
1 cup chopped button mushrooms
1 green chili, finely chopped
⅓ cup thinly sliced onion
½ tsp chili powder
¼ tsp garlic powder
1–2 tbsp chopped cilantro leaves
¼ tsp cumin seeds
¼ tsp salt
1 tbsp oil

FOOD VALUE

	TOTAL	PER PORTION (½)
TOTAL FAT	30 g	15 g
SATURATED FAT	6.7 g	3.3 g
CHOLESTEROL	658 mg	329 mg
ENERGY (calories)	378	189

METHOD

1 Separate the eggs, keeping the whites and yolks in separate containers and beating each.

2 Fold the flour into the egg yolks, together with the pepper, mushrooms, green chili, onion, and all the herbs and spices.

3 Mix the egg whites into the egg yolk mixture and beat once again, gradually adding 2 tablespoons of water.

4 Grease a large, nonstick skillet with the oil and heat it to smoking point.

5 Straight away, pour in the egg and vegetable mixture, reduce the heat and cook for 1 minute or so, shaking the pan. Then remove the pan to a hot broiler to finish cooking the omelet.

KHAGINA
A Light, Spicy Egg Dish
SERVES 2

INGREDIENTS

⅓ cup thinly sliced onion

2 green chilies, chopped

1 tbsp butter

2 tbsp julienned red bell pepper

2 cloves garlic

pinch of chili powder

pinch of salt

2 large eggs

freshly ground black pepper

2 tbsp chopped chives

FOOD VALUE

	TOTAL	PER PORTION (½)
TOTAL FAT	24.8 g	12.4 g
SATURATED FAT	11.6 g	5.8 g
CHOLESTEROL	474 mg	237 mg
ENERGY (calories)	305	153

This dish can be made in various ways. The very word "Khagina" brings back a host of wonderful memories of family get-togethers over the weekends, staying up late on Saturday nights and waking up late, starving, wanting a khagina brunch.

My husband's version is the best and he loves to watch his family fighting over it!

METHOD

1 Sweat the onion and green chilies in the butter in a nonstick skillet over a low heat for 4 to 5 minutes, adding a tiny amount of water between stirs to keep them from sticking and burning.

2 Add the red pepper and garlic and cook for 3 to 4 minutes, stirring continuously.

3 Add the chili powder, salt, and 2 tablespoons of water and let it simmer again for 2 to 3 minutes.

4 Break the eggs gently on top of the bed of vegetables and spices in the pan, taking care to keep the egg yolks intact. Shake the pan so the egg white spreads to fill the pan. Do not overcook the egg yolks – they are done when, if you were to pierce them with a fork, they would only ooze out and run slightly.

5 Grind black pepper over the top, then sprinkle the chives over and serve immediately.

BHINDI UNDA
Egg and Okra Scramble
SERVES 2

INGREDIENTS

4 oz okra
1 tbsp oil
⅓ cup chopped onion
¼ tsp cumin seeds
4 tbsp chopped tomato
pinch of turmeric
¼ tsp chili powder
½ tsp salt
freshly ground black pepper, to taste
2 tsp lemon juice
3 large eggs
3 cloves garlic, chopped
1 scallion, finely chopped

FOOD VALUE

	TOTAL	PER PORTION (½)
TOTAL FAT	31 g	15.5 g
SATURATED FAT	7 g	3.5 g
CHOLESTEROL	658 mg	329 mg
ENERGY (calories)	407	203

METHOD

1 Rinse and dry the okra well. Top and tail each one then cut it into 3 to 4 slices.

2 Heat the oil in a medium-sized nonstick skillet with a lid. Soften the onion, then add the cumin seeds.

3 Add the okra, tomato, turmeric, chili powder, and half the salt. Stir, then let the vegetables cook in their own moisture by covering the pan with its lid, over a low heat for 10 to 12 minutes, until the okra is tender. Mill some black pepper over and sprinkle in the lemon juice.

4 Break the eggs into a bowl and beat with 2 tablespoons of water. Stir in the garlic, scallion, and the remaining salt.

5 Pour the egg mixture over the vegetable mixture in the pan and, as soon as the eggs are lightly set, break up the mixture and continue to stir while it cooks. Serve immediately.

ZUCCHINI AND TOMATO RAITA

CUCUMBER AND TOMATO RELISH

SPINACH AND TOMATO RAITA

Raita

SCALLION AND CUCUMBER RAITA

EGGPLANT RAITA WITH SUNFLOWER SEEDS

All raitas make perfect salad dressings or fillings for baked potatoes, as well as serving their usual role, tasty relishes to eat with the main course. Even if you cannot afford to have a full portion caloriewise, just a couple of spoonfuls will make a big difference, enriching any meal.

There are thousands of variations that can be made on the simple basic formula of yogurt and vegetables, so try the following recipes and then let your imagination flow.

TORI RAITA
Zucchini and Tomato Raita
SERVES 4

INGREDIENTS

¼ lb baby zucchini	
2 cloves garlic, crushed	
pinch of freshly ground black pepper	
½ tsp sugar	
pinch of salt	
1 cup lowfat plain yogurt	
2 tsp mint leaves or mint sauce	
pinch of chili powder	
½ tsp cumin seeds, crushed	
2 oz tomatoes, sliced	

FOOD VALUE

	TOTAL	PER PORTION (¼)
TOTAL FAT	2.4 g	0.6 g
SATURATED FAT	1.25 g	0.3 g
CHOLESTEROL	9 mg	2 mg
ENERGY (calories)	162	40

METHOD

1 Wipe the zucchini, but do not peel. Then slice them thinly.

2 Put them into a pan with ¼ cup of slightly salted water, cover the pan and simmer for a few minutes, until the water has disappeared. Leave to cool, then mash the zucchini roughly until the last of the moisture has been absorbed.

3 Stir the crushed garlic, freshly ground black pepper to taste, the sugar, and salt into the mashed zucchini and mix together.

4 Beat the yogurt lightly until it is smooth, then pour it over the zucchini mixture.

5 Stir in the mint or mint sauce, mixing it in gently together with the yogurt.

6 Garnish the dish by "drawing" a red, brown, and black circle when you sprinkle on the chili powder, cumin seeds, and black pepper. Use the tomatoes to garnish.

Opposite:
Zucchini and Tomato Raita

Cucumber and Tomato Relish
SERVES 4

INGREDIENTS

½ lb cucumber	
2 tbsp chopped fresh mint or cilantro	
⅔ cup chopped onion	
1 tbsp vinegar or lemon juice	
1 tsp sweetened mint sauce	
salt and freshly ground black pepper, to taste	

FOOD VALUE

	TOTAL	PER PORTION (¼)
TOTAL FAT	0.4 g	0.1 g
SATURATED FAT	Tr	Tr
CHOLESTEROL	0	0
ENERGY (calories)	73	18

METHOD

1 Cut all the vegetables into either cubes or small chunks.

2 Combine the vinegar or lemon juice, mint sauce and salt and pepper.

3 Add the mint or cilantro leaves and blend all the ingredients well together. Serve chilled.

Spinach and Tomato Raita

SERVES 4

INGREDIENTS

1 cup chopped spinach

1 cup lowfat plain yogurt

pinch of chili powder

½ tsp sugar

salt and freshly ground black pepper

2 tsp oil

¼ tsp cumin seeds

¼ tsp mustard seeds (optional)

1 fat clove garlic, chopped

½ tsp grated ginger root

2 oz tomato, sliced

FOOD VALUE

	TOTAL	PER PORTION (¼)
TOTAL FAT	8.6 g	2.1 g
SATURATED FAT	1.9 g	0.5 g
CHOLESTEROL	9 mg	2 mg
ENERGY (calories)	216	54

If you decide to substitute frozen for fresh spinach, make sure it is leaf rather than pureed spinach.

METHOD

1 Rinse fresh spinach thoroughly, remove the tough stems, then chop the leaves into thin strips and drain it well. For frozen spinach, drain it well, then chop into strips as for fresh.

2 Put the spinach into a small saucepan, cover with a well-fitting lid, and cook it in its own moisture over a low heat, briefly, or until it is tender. Leave it to cool.

3 Beat the yogurt lightly in a medium-sized bowl until it is smooth and add the spinach to it. Blend in the chili powder, sugar, salt and pepper.

4 Heat the oil in a small skillet and fry the cumin and mustard seeds, if using, garlic and ginger until the seeds begin to pop (1 to 2 minutes).

5 Pour this mixture into the yogurt and spinach mixture and mix again. Garnish with the tomato and chill before serving.

PIAZ AUR KUKRI KA RAITA

Scallion and Cucumber Raita

SERVES 4

INGREDIENTS

1 cup lowfat plain yogurt

2–3 tbsp skim milk

1 cup diced cucumber

2 scallions, chopped

½ tsp sugar

salt to taste

¼ tsp Roasted and Crushed Cumin Seeds (see page 17)

pinch of chili powder

freshly ground black pepper

FOOD VALUE

	TOTAL	PER PORTION (¼)
TOTAL FAT	2.1 g	0.5 g
SATURATED FAT	1.1 g	0.3 g
CHOLESTEROL	9 mg	2 mg
ENERGY (calories)	155	39

A quick, everyday kind of raita that can be served with almost any meal.

METHOD

1 Beat the yogurt and milk lightly together in a bowl until smooth.

2 Add the cucumber, scallions, sugar, salt, and half the Cumin Seeds and mix them in well.

3 Sprinkle the chili powder over the surface of the raita in a circle, then "draw" an inner circle in the same way with the black pepper and sprinkle the remaining Cumin Seeds in the center. Alternatively, create your own patterns with these red brown and black colors.

Opposite:
Scallion and Cucumber Raita

BANGON KA RAITA
Eggplant Raita with Sunflower Seeds
SERVES 4

INGREDIENTS

1 tbsp sunflower seeds
1 cup grated eggplant
2–3 garlic cloves, crushed
pinch of salt
3–4 tbsp skim milk
1 cup lowfat plain yogurt
1 tsp artificial sugar
¼ tsp cumin seeds, crushed
¼ tsp freshly ground black pepper
⅓ cup chopped tomato
few mint leaves or pinch of dried mint
pinch of chili powder

FOOD VALUE

	TOTAL	PER PORTION (¼)
TOTAL FAT	9.6 g	2.4 g
SATURATED FAT	2.1 g	0.5 g
CHOLESTEROL	11 mg	3 mg
ENERGY (calories)	267	67

METHOD

1 Put the sunflower seeds into a heavy-bottomed skillet and heat it over a medium heat. Move the seeds around continuously with a wooden spoon, roasting them for 1 minute. Switch the heat off, but keep on shifting the seeds as the pan cools, then leave them there to cool completely.

2 Pour ¼ cup of water into a small saucepan, together with the eggplant, garlic, and a pinch of salt, then bring it to a boil. Cook for 2 to 3 minutes, until the eggplant is softened to a pulp, then remove the pan from the heat and leave it to one side to cool.

3 Beat the milk and yogurt together in a bowl until smooth, then add the eggplant, sugar, cumin seeds, and pepper and blend well.

4 Add the tomato and mint leaves or dried mint.

5 Sprinkle the chili powder over the top and garnish with the sunflower seeds just before serving.

Mango Malai

Guava and Cottage Cheese Blend

Fruit Chaat

Fruit and Yogurt Chaat

Desserts & Drinks

Tropical Fruit Salad

Lemon Drink

Yogurt Drink

Strawberry Lassi

Melon and Ginger Lassi

It is a sad fact of life that most Indian sweets are incredibly high in calories. Unlike Western sweets, however, these enormously rich and sugary sweets symbolize festivity and jubilation and so are not eaten every day but just on special occasions.

In Asian homes, we generally finish our meals with a bowl of fresh fruit as all kinds of wonderful fruits are abundant at home. Besides enjoying the fruits, the family chatter away and laugh together or discuss serious issues and so this course usually lasts much longer than the main course.

Mango Malai

SERVES 4

INGREDIENTS

½ lb fresh mango*, flesh only

1 cup lowfat plain yogurt

2–3 tbsp artificial sugar

2 tsp lemon juice

pinch of nutmeg

pinch of salt

2 oz black grapes

FOOD VALUE

	TOTAL	PER PORTION (¼)
TOTAL FAT	2.4 g	0.6 g
SATURATED FAT	1.3 g	0.3 g
CHOLESTEROL	9 mg	2 mg
ENERGY (calories)	284	71

Mango Malai is one of my favorite inventions and, if the sheer delight on the faces of my guests is anything to go by, generally extremely popular. There is a similar sweet called Aamruss, which, literally, means the mango juice, but freshly fried, delicate and light pooris are served with it which makes it less of a dessert and more like a first course.

My recipe for Mango Malai is a *bit* wicked: I use a good helping of heavy cream in it, thus the word Malai in its name, which means cream, but in trying to mend my ways, I have substituted lowfat yogurt. It is still a wonderfully refreshing dessert which has fewer calories!

METHOD

1 Put the mango, yogurt, sugar, lemon juice, nutmeg, and salt into a blender and process it until it is smooth.

2 Spoon the mixture into 4 serving dishes. Halve the grapes, discarding the seeds, if any, and decorate the dessert with them. Serve chilled.

*If you choose to use canned mango instead, the finished desserts will contain 40 more calories, or, 10 more calories per portion.

AMROOD-AFZA
Guava and Cottage Cheese Blend
SERVES 4

INGREDIENTS

1 cup cottage cheese

1 tbsp lemon juice

4 tbsp artificial sugar

2 tsp rosewater (optional)

2 tbsp skim milk

½ lb canned guavas

½ cup sliced plums

FOOD VALUE

	TOTAL	PER PORTION (¼)
TOTAL FAT	9 g	2.2 g
SATURATED FAT	5.4 g	1.3 g
CHOLESTEROL	29 mg	7 mg
ENERGY (calories)	383	96

METHOD

1 Put the cottage cheese, lemon juice, sugar, rosewater, if using, and milk into an electric blender and process until smooth.

2 Puree the guavas, together with their seeds and juices.

3 Layer the pureed guavas and cottage cheese mixtures alternately in 4 serving dishes and garnish them with the slices of plum. Serve them chilled.

Indians love sweet things. Here gur *or* jaggery, *a sweet popular with villagers, is a cheap derivative of sugar cane or palm sap, and makes a form of candy.*

Fruit Chaat

SERVES 4

INGREDIENTS

6 oz canned guavas, drained
6 oz honeydew melon
4 oz pears
4 oz apple
4 oz tangerines
¼ tsp cumin seeds, crushed
pinch of chili powder
pinch of freshly ground black pepper
pinch of salt
2–3 tsp artificial sugar
2 tbsp fresh orange juice
2 tsp lemon juice
fresh mint leaves, slightly crushed or broken, to garnish

FOOD VALUE

	TOTAL	PER PORTION (¼)
TOTAL FAT	1.3 g	0.3 g
SATURATED FAT	0	0
CHOLESTEROL	0	0
ENERGY (calories)	210	53

I am sure you will be surprised to read the list of ingredients: chili powder and salt and pepper with fruit, in a dessert? Be surprised again when you've tried it and seen for yourself how well it works.

Fruit chaats are very popular at tea parties, dinner parties, and other special occasions. They are mostly made using tropical fruits and, as the fresh ones are not always available or of the best quality, I suggest you rely on the canned ones, choosing those in their natural juices rather than syrup, and just weigh the flesh.

METHOD

1 Cut up all the fruits into small cubes or tiny segments so that the spices can mingle into the fruits easily.

2 Mix all the spices together in a bowl, pour in the sugar, orange and lemon juices, stir and shake the mixture to blend them. Pour this over the fruit, mix gently, garnish with the mint leaves and chill well before serving.

Fruit and Yogurt Chaat

SERVES 4

INGREDIENTS

4 oz canned guavas, drained

4 oz canned pineapple, drained

1 banana

1 cup lowfat plain yogurt

2–3 tbsp artificial sugar

2 tsp lemon juice

pinch of coarse salt

pinch of freshly ground black pepper

pinch of cardamom pods, crushed, or pinch of grated nutmeg

2 oz pomegranate, flesh only, or 3 oz fresh cherries

FOOD VALUE

	TOTAL	PER PORTION (¼)
TOTAL FAT	3 g	0.8 g
SATURATED FAT	1.1 g	0.3 g
CHOLESTEROL	9 mg	2 mg
ENERGY (calories)	347	87

METHOD

1 Cut all the fruit – except the pomegranate – into bite-size pieces.

2 Beat the yogurt briefly until it is smooth.

3 Add the sugar, lemon juice, salt, pepper, and cardamom or nutmeg to the yogurt and mix them together well.

4 Add the fruit to the yogurt and mix them in gently. Divide the mixture between 4 serving dishes. Scatter the pomegranate like pearls over each dish and chill well before serving.

Fruits and fruit juices are the perfect companions to spicy Indian food.

Tropical Fruit Salad

SERVES 4

INGREDIENTS

½ lb mango flesh

6 oz honeydew melon

4 oz kiwi fruit

5 oz canned lychees

2 tbsp orange juice

2 tsp lemon juice

1 tbsp artificial sugar

FOOD VALUE

	TOTAL	PER PORTION (¼)
TOTAL FAT	1.2 g	0.3 g
SATURATED FAT	0.3 g	Tr
CHOLESTEROL	0	0
ENERGY (calories)	373	93

METHOD

1 Cut the mango into bite-size cubes.

2 Use a melon baller to cut out as many little balls as possible from the melon.

3 Peel and slice the kiwi fruit.

4 Drain the lychees.

5 Mix the orange and lemon juices and sugar together and pour this over the fruit. Mix well and chill.

6 Just before serving, divide the fruit between 4 serving dishes and top each one with whole lychees.

NIMBOO PAANI
Lemon Drink
SERVES 1

INGREDIENTS

juice of ½ lemon

1¼ cups water

2–3 tbsp artificial sugar

ice cubes as required

*fresh mint leaves and lemon wedges
to garnish*

The literal translation is "lemon water" and it is an equally popular drink in both India and Pakistan. It is made in more or less the same way in Pakistan but goes under the name of Skunjbeen.

No cooking is involved – it is simply made from fresh lemon juice and sugar. If you replace the real sugar with artificial sugar you have "Diet Nimboo Paani" in a matter of minutes. The best part is that you could drink gallons of it without consuming a single calorie. Also, if you drink it during or after a meal it is doubly beneficial – it helps you to enjoy the meal and, at the same time, takes away the urge for a dessert. Drink it between meals if you are feeling peckish for no reason and it will melt your hunger away, as well as giving you plenty of Vitamin C.

METHOD

1 Put all but the garnishing ingredients into an electric blender and blend for a few seconds.

2 Pour into a tall glass and garnish with the mint leaves and lemon wedges.

LASSI
Yogurt Drink
SERVES 2

INGREDIENTS

½ cup lowfat plain yogurt

2½ cups water

2–3 tbsp artificial sugar

ice cubes as required

pinch of salt

4 mint leaves to garnish (optional)

FOOD VALUE

	TOTAL	PER PORTION (½)
TOTAL FAT	3.2 g	1.6 g
SATURATED FAT	2 g	1 g
CHOLESTEROL	16 mg	8 mg
ENERGY (calories)	224	112

A delicious, cooling and most satisfying drink. Once you try it, you can easily get hooked on it and, in hot weather, it is almost like an answer to one's prayer! Nothing else quenches your thirst quite the way lassi does.

A small glass of sweet lassi can be served as a liquid dessert, especially following a spicy meal.

Lassi does not necessarily have to be sweet; savory versions are also very popular – try one with a pinch of salt and leave the sugar out, freshly ground black pepper and chopped mint leaves for slightly spicy taste. Try them and see which one is for you.

METHOD

1 Put all the ingredients, except the mint leaves, into an electric blender (or use a hand-held blender) and blend thoroughly until it becomes frothy.

2 Pour it into a tall glass and add some more ice cubes if you wish. Garnish with the mint leaves, if using, and serve immediately. (If you leave it undrunk for too long, the yogurt separates and rises to the surface, leaving the water underneath it, but all you have to do is just stir it to amalgamate them once more.)

Strawberry Lassi
SERVES 1

INGREDIENTS

¼ cup lowfat plain yogurt

3 oz fresh or frozen strawberries

1–2 tbsp artificial sugar

ice cubes as required

scant 2 cups water

FOOD VALUE

	TOTAL	PER SERVING
TOTAL FAT	0.5 g	0.5 g
SATURATED FAT	0.25 g	0.25 g
CHOLESTEROL	2 mg	2 mg
ENERGY (calories)	48	48

METHOD

1 Put all the ingredients in an electric blender and blend for 30 seconds.

2 Pour into a tall glass, adding more ice cubes if you like.

125

Melon and Ginger Lassi

SERVES 1

INGREDIENTS

¼ cup lowfat plain yogurt

3 oz melon flesh

½ tsp ground ginger

1–2 tbsp artificial sugar

ice cubes as required

scant 1 cup water

FOOD VALUE

	TOTAL	PER SERVING
TOTAL FAT	0.5 g	0.5 g
SATURATED FAT	0.25 g	0.25 g
CHOLESTEROL	2 mg	2 mg
ENERGY (calories)	42	42

METHOD

1 Put all the ingredients into an electric blender and blend until the mixture is frothy.

2 Pour into a tall glass and drop in some more ice if you like.

Index

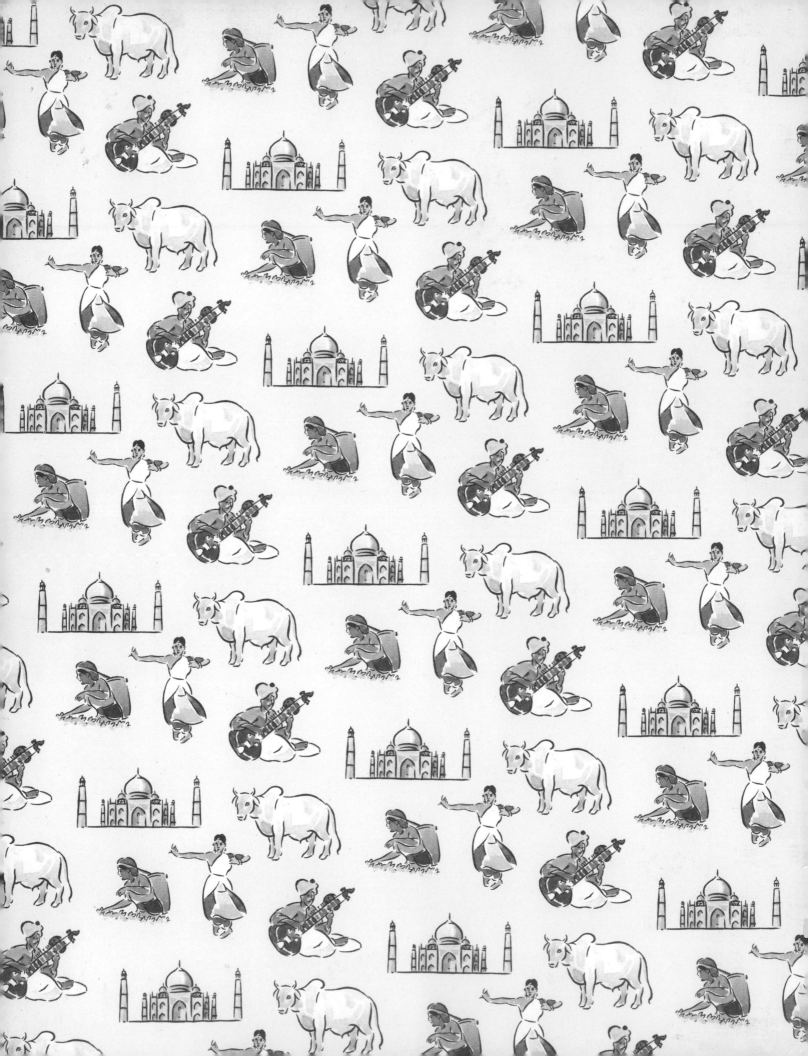